BREAK FREE

To Peace, Love & Unity

Compiled by Seema Giri
#1 International Best Selling Author

My Dear Susan -
You were the one who gave me
the Courage to write my story
when we met - I'm grateful for
you and all you do.
I love you so much,
Sharon

Break Free
To Peace, Love & Unity

Uplyft Media
5922 Rosewood Road
Dublin CA 94568.

ISBN 978-1-7350255-2-0

ACKNOWLEDGMENTS

Life has unfolded in very surprising ways for me, presenting me with opportunities that I would never have imagine. I was quite content as an entrepreneur in the project management domain, where I had the privilege of equipping organizations with knowledge, processes, and tools to adapt and grow in an environment of a continuous state of change, making a direct impact on the organization's strategic objectives while empowering the people.

Little did I know that the universe would grant me the honor of even higher service to bring forth a collection of real-life, extraordinarily intimate, and introspective stories that will change your views or perception of life as you know it. I am grateful for the courage to forge forward on this new exciting path and lean into stepping out of my comfort zone.

To my family. My husband, Upendra: for always being the person I could turn to for encouragement and advice when I was not sure how to move forward. Especially for the endless times of feeding me breakfast, lunch, and dinner in my office. To my son, Aman, who is never amazed at my achievements as he expects me to reach them effortlessly. I find great comfort in his certainty of my capabilities. To my daughter, Ashima, who leads by example of bravery and is my inspiration to become the best version of myself. Her pandemic life started a year and a half earlier than the rest of the world when she had a near-death experience when she flipped her car sideways and walked away with some scratches and glass in her hand. No matter what was going on, she always made sure to make her special Ashi Baby coffee for me. I am truly blessed.

Thanks to everyone on the publishing and editing team. Especially Atul and Natasha from the graphics team for the numerous iterations until we got the perfect book cover and images. To Rebecca, for holding the space and guidance to create this beautiful masterpiece.

I am grateful to the amazing group of collaborators, the co-authors who entrusted me to bring forward their powerful stories of breaking free to empowerment. Writing about the story of your life is a difficult and surreal process. Their stories are a work of deep reflection and storytelling, where they invite the readers into their world, describing their triumphs and disappointments that have shaped their lives to explore the opportunities to ultimately *Break Free to Peace, Love, and Unity*.

Finally, I want to thank you, the reader, for leaning into these stories that will touch your heart and soul in profound ways. Allow yourself to embrace the gifts of love, wisdom, and hope that will enrich your life's experience.

CONTENTS

PART 1: BREAK FREE

THE CALL THAT CHANGED MY LIFE
BY KAREN WRIGHT

It was a warm September day. I had just gotten done with my second-oldest daughter's orchestra class. The music was spellbinding as the group of thirty kids played Disney music with enthusiasm and gusto. Marae's half-grin told me as she sat next to me in the passenger seat that she was on point as the teacher cued her section in. My daughter was going places. My mind wondered as I pictured her on stage, her dashing long red hair flowing over her electric violin as her bow blazed across her strings. My four kids amazed me, and each had a talent that fit them. I was the cheerleader, making sure "my" dreams of what I envisioned for them would come true. ***Yes, I knew they might not all agree with my desires for them, yet I could not stop dreaming for them. My dreams were but a distant memory. At a young age, I became a wife and mom. No longer did my dreams matter; at least, that was what I thought.***

Turning out of the parking lot and heading toward home, I picked up the phone and dialed my husband to see how our senior in high school did at her first cross-country race of the season.

The phone rang several more times than usual before Grady answered with a tone I had never heard in my eighteen years of marriage. "Karen, I can't talk right now."

The phone was silent. Concern overtook my body, and I swerved my SUV into an abandoned lot, my hands sweating on the steering wheel, as I pushed redial.

Grady picked up after the first ring. "Karen, Kalena had a seizure at the race, and I am taking her to the hospital. Meet me there."

One phone call, and my life was altered forever.

Oh, how I wish I could tell you that my daughter was okay. But I cannot.

Kalena, our oldest daughter, left this earthly life on the way to the hospital that day. Never in my wildest dreams did I ever think I would ever bury my own child. Five days later, with anguish and pain written all over me, I gave her body to mother earth; her spirit already entered heaven.

How does a mother, father, parent live with the death of a child? Everyone is different, and there is no right way to handle such a situation. I cried, yelled at God, slept, kept to myself, and got on an antidepressant to help with my agony. I was a mom with three living children, and I learned quickly how to survive. **I buried my emotions deep inside and tended to my kids. I was needed. And I was determined to help ease their hurt and sorrow as much as I could. At my darkest hour, I came to realize that I no longer knew who I was. I felt I had died with my daughter.**

On the surface, I wore the labels as a wife, mom, maid, taxi driver—you name it, I wore the label. But these were titles I had allowed others to put on me. Society, environment, upbringing, and religious beliefs each had their effect on my character. Deep down, I was lost. At the moment Kalena was given to the earth, I had a solemn awakening that I had lived my life through my kids and stamps that had been carefully attached to me without me knowing.

The day at Kalena's gravesite, the sky was filled with gray clouds; it looked so heavy, just like my heart felt. Family and friends gathered in a circle, each holding balloons. As the balloons were let go, the clouds parted, and the sun's golden rays glowed across the azure sky. I was smiling as a tear moistened my cheek. I realized I was chained to markers that kept me bound to false labels and expectations that had been placed on me. I decided then I would no longer claim this marker as "me." I cut and released the chain. As the balloons drifted toward the opening sky, I realized that I no longer wanted to be caged. It was my time to soar.

My journey began over sixteen years ago. The death of Kalena was my wake-up call. I was in a relationship with a man who was very successful in the material world and knew what he wanted and made sure he got what he desired. Being married at a young age to a controlling, emotional, and verbal man, I never saw how he manipulated situations to make sure he won at the end of the day. **As I matured and started to gain a voice and opinions, my man soon categorized me as a bitch and self-centered.**

I am a Pisces; we fish are here to help others, and in helping others, I became a chameleon, adapting to each environment that needed me. Yes, I was a pleaser—a giver. I continued to do my best with the requests my husband had asked me to do. Over time, I realized that no matter what I did for my husband, it would never be enough.

This "ah-ha" moment played out in my laundry room as I folded clothes and read the new stencil I had only a month earlier put on the wall. It said, "Wash Today, OR Naked Tomorrow!" My mind raced. Clothes always felt binding to me. I loved being in my birthday suit whenever I could. But with four kids, a husband, and neighborhood friends entering our home without a knock, the nakedness did not manifest very often. I longed to be able to leave the clothes in the basket and walk away, no longer having the desire to wear clothing. **Freedom was in the air, and as my squirrel mind raced, I understood that no matter how often I washed and folded clothes, it would never end. The end of doing all I could to please my husband would also never end.** Just when I thought I had accomplished the task he had placed on me exactly how he wanted it, I soon realized he would change his mind and want it a different way. Or better yet, he would come up with a completely new idea he wanted me to fulfill. It was never-ending, just like the wash—constantly in your face as a reminder that I never succeeded.

As I stood looking at my quote on the beige wall, I made up my mind to stop trying to please my husband. I would do what he asked, but I would do things my way, and I would learn quickly not to care if it upset him. Either way, he would be mad. But I would be free to choose how I felt after I accomplished the task at hand. A weight lifted off my shoulders that day, and I stood a little taller. My step was lighter, and I felt a spark inside me that I had not felt since I was a young girl.

As a tomboy, I loved nature. I grew up in Washington with a green forest out of my childhood home. Most days, you could find me running wild, playing war games, climbing trees, building jumps for my bike, and making pine-needle forts. I loved the smell, the taste of pine—all of it was magical to me. **Now, as an adult, I found my trail that took me home to my youth.** With my pups in tow daily, we make the trek as I walk side by side along the babbling creek that runs year-round to keep my dogs from dry mouths. This time in nature truly kept me sane after the loss of my daughter. **I began to talk out loud to God. He always listened to me and never interrupted. He continued to be by my side as I yelled at him, cried to him, and shared my innermost feelings with him. Not once did God judge me or put labels on me. He loves the authentic, crazy goddess that I am.**

As the hike takes me back down the mountain trail, my mind usually calms, and then I listen. Yes, God speaks to me in my language and in a way that makes sense to my simple nature. And I then take his advice and let things happen that are in the plan God has for me. For many years, I thought I knew what I needed in my life and what would make me happy. **The day God took Kalena from me, I realized that I am not the captain of my ship; God is. No matter the conditions of the water, whether it's calm, rough, or storming, God will help us get through them if we learn to "let go and let God."** This is another saying I have hanging on my bathroom wall. This "letting go" has been one of my hardest lessons on faith that I have ever experienced. Once I put my ego in the back seat and allow God to work his magic, my life seems to flow. Don't be fooled—even with God in control, there are still ups and downs as I ride the waves of my ocean. The cool thing is that they are my waves, my learning experiences, my truths.

One truth I have learned while living my adventures is that I am meant to fly. For most of my life, I was caged with beliefs and influenced by my environment and loved ones on how I should live my life. Once I allowed myself to open the door to my cage and stepped forward and flap my wings, another remarkable "ah-ha" moment happened. **God has given me intelligence, and with my knowledge, I can make my own choices and allow what happens to follow.**

My choices have led me to new forms of healing and finding the love, peace, and unity within me. One summer, I spent a month in Bali by myself, becoming yoga certified. Never in my young fifty-three years had I flown halfway across the world without anyone with me. I was alone and truly bubbling inside with excitement for this month-long adventure I had decided to take. The time in Bali brought awareness to the new me. **For the first time in my life, I could look in the mirror and see me for me. I loved every inch of my body—my scars, my loose skin, my lines that caressed my smile and eyes. Gratitude filled me as I thanked God for the woman I had become.**

With this newfound love of yoga, I began to learn more about the energy chakras that are inside each of us. My questions about the chakras began to grow as I googled articles and read about these amazing vortexes we each are born with. I did not understand why such glorious energy was seldom talked about in the western world. But eastern medicine had been aware of these balls of energy for thousands of years. With my reading, I came across an article on reiki. It is known as a Japanese form of alternative medicine called energy healing. Reiki practitioners use a technique called palm healing or hands-on healing through which a "universal energy" is said to be transferred through the palms of the practitioner to the patient in order to encourage emotional or physical healing.

Soon, I found a local reiki master that taught the Usui-Holy Fire Reiki. With her guidance and direction in the art of Holy Fire Reiki, **I became a master and began another journey of healing clients. My light inside of me was shining brightly, and my path continues to lead me in a direction that allows love, peace, and unity within my spirit and soul.**

I believe each of us has a mission here on this earth. Now is the time to love all of you, never ignoring yourself again. I have made a vow to myself to never divorce myself again. I love the woman I have become, and I will continue to evolve along my path. I know that each of us can achieve what God has planned for us as we follow our own path and enjoy the adventures our journey will take us on.

May you fully love who you are and let your light shine powerfully and brightly to the world. Peace, love, and unity start from within each of us. We must first have peace and love all of ourselves, and then we can shine it out into the world.

Karen Wright

Once upon a time, Karen Wright completely lost all aspects of herself: heart, mind, body, and soul—until the unexpected death of her precious eighteen-year-old daughter awakened her to the fact that she herself had never truly lived.

Her book, *Now or Never: Shine Baby Shine*, honors powerful and tender lessons from her daughter, inspiring Karen's adventure to rediscover and reclaim her very identity and her powerful light.

Karen is now a passionate author, speaker, trainer, yoga instructor, and savvy businesswoman who has built a thriving real estate career in the midst of her journey.

Through self-development, fine-tuning meditation skills, and being carried by God, Karen walks her readers and clients through all of the inevitable turns, hills, and valleys of life's unexpected journeys.

Karen has a dynamic personality and zest for life; she has helped her audiences through her many speaking engagements by being authentic and vulnerable by telling her personal journey's loss and pain and rising to her higher self.

Karen is now best known for living life as an adventure. A nature lover and incredibly active, daily you will find her hiking with her two puppies in the mountains or snow-skiing or waterskiing with her kids, as well as many other physical and spiritual adventures. Karen lives her truths, and with her understanding and sense of humor, she welcomes others into her tribe with open arms.

Discover your deepest authenticity and find out who you really are.

Email: **Skibumwright@gmail.com**
Phone: 1-801-695-2378
Website: **https://www.yourbestmoveyet.net/**
Author Domain: **shinenowornever.com**
Facebook: **https://www.facebook.com/kwhouseforyou**
Instagram: **https://www.instagram.com/shinenowornever/**

THE VOICE
BY LAUREL HARRIS

There's a voice in my head. It's constant and compelling; some might say, relentless. I hear it. The question is, do I listen?

Okay, in all honesty, there's more than one voice at any given time, and my guess is that they're pretty similar to yours.

Fortunately, as an actor, getting to know these voices is highly regarded since we creatives rely on any number of them to build the characters we bring to life.

We, and you, the audience, want these characters to seamlessly integrate themselves into the elaborate stories being told, so we take our job of creating new and exciting art that reflects the world we all inhabit very seriously.

We build these characters from the ground up, so to speak.

We research and extract information from ourselves and others as if it were precious gemstones being forged from rugged rocks within the earth's crumbly crust. As these newly formed beings, aka characters, begin to take shape, they can feel quite precious as we try them on for size and inhabit them for any length of time, a second skin of sorts.

We eventually breathe and eat and laugh and create vivid life experiences through and for them, and we (hopefully) call it "fun!"

How do we do it? By observing humanity with keen attention and intention. We put ourselves and others under a microscope and dissect what we most want to learn.

Ideally, this isn't to harm others in any way but to gratefully receive the information they give us so we can go back to the lab and build a new being.

We hear the myriad of voices—ours and those we interact with, and we lean in. **Listening becomes an art form.**

Fortunately, decades of this critical character analysis has taught me much. Though one lesson stands above the rest: listening isn't only vital for actors but for humanity as a whole.

As Shakespeare so poignantly reminds us, "All the world's a stage, and all the men and women merely players." I'll take the liberty of adding to Sir Will by asking, therefore, shouldn't we all be actively listening to one another?

According to Oxford Living Dictionaries, "to listen is to give attention to sound or action. When listening, one is hearing what others are saying and trying to understand what it means. The act of listening involves complex affective, cognitive, and behavioral processes."

I think with the endless distractions our current world provides that it's time to increase our capacity to truly listen to ourselves and each other if we want to elevate our present climate and find lasting peace, love, and unity, both within ourselves and each other.

With full respect to the scientific definitions, **I believe deep, honest, and active listening involves giving our undivided attention with more than just our ears. It requires us to let go of the varied voices and tune in.**

It sounds like a tall order, yet I've learned the results ultimately award more successful and joyful life endeavors. In other words, there really is more to this than meets the ear.

This is where it gets real, and I'll start with a confession.

I do hear all of the voices in my head—often more than I'd like, to be honest—but there's one voice that takes precedent: "THE" voice. While it's rather quiet and unassuming in stature (i.e., it's not winning awards for belting bravado at the Met), I've known it well and have been "conversing" with it long before I was verbal.

We've bantered and bickered and gone through the paces together, and ultimately, this voice always wins. (Actually, for the record, I'm the only one bantering and bickering, as it's a superior sensei and has yet to argue with me in any way, mean, or fashion.) Does it challenge me? Without question. Will it ever argue? Not a chance.

This voice is unique. It's unlike any one of the myriads of archetypal ones that I look to when coloring in a vivid character. And, while a concoction of these voices may be preening for my attention at any given time, I've learned to separate and lovingly shush them.

I've become emboldened by recognizing the ones that are attached to survival or want to be cherished or to be forever right.

Now I can call out my inner toddler that might be adorable one moment, yet plead with me to flail about loudly and obnoxiously, demand attention, and seek a focal point on which to purge some occasional outbursts and temper tantrums immediately thereafter.

I also know there's a frightened inner critic that wants me to passionately react with lightning speed to every curveball and unsuspected situation that arises, especially the unpleasant ones. There are the sympathy laden, whiny voice and the fierce fighter with killer boots and a perfectly billowed cape. I'm also well aware of the victim, and the hero, and the suspect and the . . . well, you get the point. They all relentlessly vie for my attention. Perhaps you can relate.

Thankfully, that's not the voice I'm talking about—not the one I call "THE."

Instead of talking at me, THE voice deeply listens to me and for me with a gentle presence, a trusted confidant of sorts. Ultimately passionate about my thriving, it lets me take as much time as I need while patiently waiting for me to finish talking, whispering, begging, crying, screaming, asking, or pleading with it for any number of reasons.

If listening had a face, I imagine THE voice would have a permanent, slight, and ever-intriguing, Buddha-like smile. It might crack a toothy grin on rare occasions over my entertaining dramatics, but it will always look at me with such intense, calm loving that I never question its motives.

Always conspiring in my favor, it desires nothing more than for my life to be wildly brilliant and ecstatic in every way possible; certainly beyond anything I could comprehend.

Luckily, it's only taken me a few dozen years or so to realize this, but who's counting?

Now, I can hear you asking at this point, "Why would you ever disagree with, or question, THE voice? Why not honor its beautiful wisdom-within 24/7?" There's a simple answer to that: I'm stubborn.

From the time I was two years old and dramatically stomped my foot at my mother because I wanted to go out in a snowstorm without shoes (a memory I don't recall but never lived down), I get that I often want my own way.

Even though my patient mother finally gave in, and even though I promptly changed my mind within minutes of my tiny feet blushing plum-red, perhaps my inner toddler still thinks this is the way to win door prizes for best actress in a real-life drama?

Or perhaps, I admit, it's because asking THE voice which kind of toothpaste to buy couldn't possibly go toe-to-toe in the quality comparisons category with asking which turn I should take on my career path next? Somehow the fluoride-free question seems irrelevant in scope to the "shall I uproot my life and move across the country for work" question, all things considered equal.

And yet, here's the catch: the questions are not different, after all! There are no irrational, stupid, or irrelevant questions, and they're all intensely valued, no matter the "category" in the world of my inner voice. Anything I present must be viewed equally because it all serves the same purpose: to get me to *listen*! Ahhh, yes. That golden acting trait that applies to all the world's "players," I now realize must start from within.

So, if the first lesson is to hear our inner voices, then the second step must be to earnestly listen to them. And if there were some spectacular scorekeeper in the sky tallying up, we'd get extra credit points for listening to THE voice within most of all. That one that sounds like "out of the blue," or "from nowhere" and my favorite, "the craziest coincidence." Yeah, that one.

At this point, I'll admit that I've gotten better at prioritizing THE voice with the Buddha-like smile and calming demeanor for toothpaste truths because I know it speaks for my highest good, and ultimately the greatest good of others too.

The challenge then becomes: do I have the courage to hear, listen, and then *follow* that voice, as the final step in my suggested equation? Well, let's just say that making those minor and "more involved" life decisions gets that much sweeter when I do.

It's a simple answer, right? Yes, it's simple. It's just not always easy. Remember, I never said those other voices weren't convincing. I'm an actor, and I know a good performance when I hear it. And, if they aren't winning me over, then there's always money, fame, fortune, or relationship issues potentially attached to these archetype's arguments to honey the taunt. Their glitzy demeanor can lure me with dazzling seduction if I'm not paying attention.

Fortunately, my experiences of following THE voice remind me of the inherent, inevitable rewards. THE voice has guided me down surprising side streets to avoid car crashes and traffic delays or led me into high demand, primo parking spots with eye-opening ease.

It's allowed the perfect words (that clearly were not "mine") to fall out of my mouth for another listener to savor in their painful life moments, or kept my mouth sealed shut so as not to recklessly throw verbal jabs I would later regret.

THE voice has helped me mend teetering relationships with family and nudged me to accept auditions and job offers I was certain would never amount to much, then later watched them turn into roles in major films, television shows, or commercial campaigns that ran for years when they were originally slated to last a fraction of that time.

Yes, THE voice has physically moved me across multiple states to live with people I never expected to see, let alone live with, and invited me to share life-changing journeys with folks I thought were on my "now or never" list.

It's even said "yes" to me taking skydiving for a spin—a choice we, or I, later had a very heated discussion about as I attempted to gulp my heart out of my throat and back into my chest where it belonged upon landing.

All the while, as these experiences have unfolded for me, and I've leaned forward into THE voice, rather than backpedal or stomp my little foot, or run for the hills like I might have literally done once, or countless times, I've noticed one thing.

This one voice not only exists within all of us, it continually, unceasingly, also beckons us toward truth. It knows the answers, my answers and your answers, which are ultimately all the same: to find and create lasting peace, love, and unity for ourselves, as well as for the lives of those around us.

Any character I see in this adventure called "Life," whether it be one I'm building or observing, has shown me that THE voice is just as peaceful, connected, wise, or comedic within every being it inhabits. No question.

Of course, **we each have the ability to hear, listen, and follow THE voice within; the trick is always, are we ready and willing to tune in?**

When I imagine a world where true listening abounds, miracles seem that much more accessible. They brilliantly pop and percolate all around us. Can you hear them?

I imagine a most inviting path to peace, love, and unity able to unfurl before us because our focused listening accelerates. Can you see it?

I believe it's possible to find more peace when we turn off those body appendages attached to the outsides of our heads and really tune in. I think we can learn to listen from the vital organ pumping in our chests and let it help us to find more love. Can you feel it?

To experience more unity with ourselves and humanity, I believe in our ability to take bold and courageous actions toward leaning inward and then outward.

Maybe even more of us can "listen" from the space between our eyebrows, that some would call our third eye, and see if it has anything to offer us? I think it's possible—if we only hear it, listen, and then follow.

So, are you listening?

Laurel Harris

Laurel Harris is an award-winning producer and American actress best known as Willem Dafoe's wife in the screen adaptation of Dean Koontz's bestselling novel, *Odd Thomas*, and loved by young girls worldwide for the American Girl film, *Saige Paints the Sky*, opposite Jane Seymour. Her extensive TV credits include ABC, NBC, CW, and Disney, and feature films with STARZ, Paramount, and Fusion. As a producer, Laurel has garnered an EMMY from the Heartland Chapter as well as multiple NATOA and TELLY Awards. She's worked with many notable figures, including Nobel Peace Laureates Archbishop Desmond Tutu and His Holiness the Dalai Lama while traveling the world to film their stories and work alongside teams from the BBC and PBS. During these adventures, Laurel developed a passion for creating media that highlights underserved populations under her Laurel Leaf Productions banner.

Laurel is a contributing writer for *ThriveGlobal* and *Backstage* magazines, as well as a respected voiceover artist, voicing countless television and radio commercials, along with numerous feature-length documentaries. Laurel's narrations in the *Nobel Legacy Film Series* premiered for two consecutive years at the Venice International Film Festival. The documentaries *SHIRIN EBADI: UNTIL WE ARE FREE* and *THE DALAI LAMA - SCIENTIST*—which received a standing ovation from a standing-room-only crowd—have received international critical acclaim.

Email: **laurel@laurelleafproductions.com**
Website: **www.laurelharris.com**
Facebook: **https://www.facebook.com/laurelharrisact**
LinkedIn: **www.linkedin.com/in/laurelharrisactor**
Twitter: **https://twitter.com/laurelharrisact**
YouTube: **https://youtube.com/channel/UC5GxLPQ4vK93UJEq6Vu_VxQ**
Instagram: **https://www.instagram.com/laurelharrisactor/**

ONE RECOVERING ACTIVIST'S SEARCH FOR PEACE, LOVE & UNITY

BY ARIEL BICKEL

"Light is not selfish, it shines on everything."
—Mooji

I stared, transfixed at the flames of the campfire as they quickly consumed the old work documents, first nibbling at the edges with curiosity, then swallowing them up in one huge gulp, hungrily transforming the once-seemingly-important papers back into raw energy.

The intensity of the ceremonial fire reflected the pain in my chest as I felt my heart breaking. Thinking about all the time, effort, and belief I'd invested in this career, my ego raged and trembled and wept. I felt so alone, defeated, inadequate.

I felt exhausted, too. Disillusioned and angry at myself for failing to inspire people, organizations, and ultimately society, to want to change:

Had anything I'd done in my life up till now even mattered?

There was no turning back now. I had hit the wall. For real. For good this time. I simply wasn't willing to sacrifice one more day of my life, grinding myself into the ground in order to vanquish the demons of this world. I was done trying to earn my right to be alive, to prove that I'm worthy of love, by martyring myself. It was time to find a new, easier, more nurturing, and joyful way to bring about greater Peace, Love, and Unity on the planet.

Hi, my name is Ariel, and I'm a recovering Activist, *Helper, and Fixer.*

I've spent the last thirty years trying to eradicate pain and injustice from the face of the earth in hopes that no other person would ever experience the trauma, abuse, and rejection that I experienced growing up. TWENTY TWENTY was the first year that I completely let go of doing activism and political work, which had been my economic mainstay and passion for the past three decades of my life.

This was an extremely intentional decision and one that took me a few years to muster up the courage to follow through on 100 percent. I've run the gamut of emotions, from elated and liberated, to terrified and self-doubting. Certainly, the pandemic has brought these huge life lessons and insights into intense focus and provoked even more powerful, rapid shifts than I originally anticipated.

Saniel Bonder, in his book, *Waking Down*, calls this phase "the Rot," and Ram Dass refers to it as "becoming nobody." You also may hear it referred to as *identity death*, *ego death*, *the dark night of the soul*, or *awakening to the Self*.

These are all ways to describe the transcending of the ego and blossoming connection with the true Self (consciousness), which isn't controlled or limited by the fears, boundaries, or expectations of our identity or persona.

The Self is a pure manifestation of our fundamental nature, including connectedness, love, and compassion.

It's the ego that tries to keep itself viable and alive by generating false separations among us and others. Ego recognizes and perpetuates the idea of "the other." Ego, along with its sidekick, the mind, invents and feeds off our insecurities, doubts, grief, need for love, judgments, worries of the small self, and other survival impulses. When we're living from a place of ego, rather than our true Self, we are ruled by these things.

What does an identity unraveling have to do with the theme of Peace, Love, and Unity? Here's what I've come to understand about creating a world rooted in Peace, Love, and Unity: *it's an inside job.*

The Peace, Love, and Unity we wish to see in the world must first be realized within each of us, *by us*.

We must come to know ourselves as the very embodiment of these gifts and share them with intention so that others feel inspired and compelled to wake up to their own potential as loving beings.

No person, place, or thing outside of us has the ability to grant us the love, acceptance, and sense of belonging that we deeply yearn for.

No amount of material possessions, degrees, promotions, or awards can provide us with the self-esteem and confidence we lack.

No social status, political title, electoral outcome, or vast business empire can guarantee the safety, longevity, or happiness that we aspire to.

To set ourselves completely free, we get to first realize that we're *already free*. We get to relax our harsh judgment of ourselves, learning to integrate and love all of our parts, including the dark aspects of our personalities (the ***shadow self***) that we fear to acknowledge. As we connect with this greater Self, we begin letting go of our need to control, manipulate, bully, or judge anyone else in order to feel safe. We understand that our own fears and darkness are what we truly fear, and that others only have the power over us which we give them.

We drop our need to view people as "the other" in order to protect ourselves, and begin to accept responsibility for our own lives, including our emotions.

We stop camouflaging our shame and guilt by blaming others for all the problems in our lives and the world.

We learn to trust ourselves and life as it unfolds, without needing to whip ourselves into perfect productivity-bots in order to compete with and prove ourselves to others.

No amount of hustling, crushing it, grinding, pushing through, demanding perfection, criticizing and judging, punishing, depriving, overworking, or holding expectations is going to perpetuate an environment of Love, Peace, and Unity.

Peace, Love, Unity—we talk about them like they're rare gems, we stalk them like they're elusive prey, we even commercialize them in the self-help and activist worlds by selling them as if they were limited commodities. But they're readily available, free to all of us who choose to sit still long enough to access them within.

No amount of legislating, spending, threatening, chasing, manipulating, or begging can command their presence.

It's not typically until we come face to face with life's inevitable challenges and suffering that we begin to question the deeper meaning of them. The pandemic is a classic example of this axiom.

As I venture deeper into my own journey of self-awareness, I witness my perception of my past shifting greatly, and my willingness and ability to accept life as it's showing up to be growing stronger.

I've been reflecting upon how I colluded with old paradigms (aka ways of thinking) and their superficial fixes in order to create the illusion of a world without trauma and suffering. This I did knowingly (though not always quietly or joyfully), and also unconsciously because my traumatized inner child-ego was trying desperately to both heal and avoid her pain by focusing on fixing or curing others'.

The past year was an eye-opening, humbling awakening to new levels of self-understanding, surrender, acceptance, forgiveness, and repatterning.

One such revelation came during a two-day meditation retreat where we spent time in meditation and openhearted conversations about the ways in which we're holding ourselves back and playing small. After one of the meditations, I got the chance to address the issue directly with the facilitator...

He helped me to see the truth of how I've spent my life trying to prove my worthiness and usefulness by working myself into the ground in order to "save the world." **This has been a way for me to be seen, gain some kind of recognition, and feel I was part of a family of like-minded people.**

Adult life replicates our childhoods. Any group setting—office, organization, classroom, friends, clients—may possess elements of our family-of-origin dynamic. Unconscious learned and inherited beliefs, biases, and patterns play out among the members of these groups; an office, for example, can be a positive place of collaboration and friendships, or a tense, punitive, and highly competitive arena.

There's a common misconception that because philanthropic, nonprofit, activist, and political foundations, movements, organizations, and campaigns committed to social justice are established with the intention to serve and support positive change, that somehow they're exempt from the pitfalls of ego. Often, the positive public images of such institutions mask deeply divided, unstable, and dysfunctional internal systems.

There are also prevailing messages which beginning activists and organizers often receive: be prepared to be on-call, work seven days a week, and/or long hours; don't expect to make money, *saving the world is its own reward*; we're one, we're all connected, so love everyone, *except for those evil people who are ruining the world*; we're the good guys, with high morals and ethics, so *we're justified in doing whatever it takes to make sure we win.*

We're trained to selflessly serve from a depleted cup without ever addressing our own needs. We forget to include ourselves in the humanity we're working so tirelessly to help.

Politics and activism are high-stakes arenas, and the pressure to "change the world," win, bring in money, and build power and influence, are constant.

For years, this high level of anxiety and sacrifice felt exciting, challenging, important, and even comfortable. I grew up in a household that was unpredictable, chaotic, and violent; there was so much about the traditional "old paradigm" activist world that resonated with my body, mind, and emotions.

This is why, in my quest to go deeper and clear out old energy from my years as an activist, I started developing a practice of meditating, tapping (EFT), and radical gratitude. It was during one particular session that I was shocked to realize that I was still hanging on to unresolved anger about people who I believed had hurt me, and that I still wanted them to suffer so I could justify living from a victim space.

In this moment, I tasted what forgiveness and compassion could feel like, for my wounded inner child, and for others...

What could true freedom feel like if I just allowed myself to lay down my judgments, assumptions, and need to be right anymore?

I had spent so many years judging and blaming people and factors outside of myself for my rage at the world, and justified my tactics, words, and actions by buying into the belief that "this is just the ways things are, this is what you have to do to get things done, to win."

In my gut, I'd known that I was living out of alignment, but at the time, I truly believed that that was the only way to make positive change in the world.

I now know that those outward behaviors, those patterns, attitudes, and beliefs, weren't really who I *am*. They were just costumes I'd been wearing for years, but hadn't realized were too tight.

My desire to belong, as well as feel engaged and needed, lead me further and further away from myself and my life became very small.

Political, social, and familial groups can easily morph into polarized, defensive, destructive forces. It's our egoic identity of specialness and invincibility, separateness, and boundaryless self-sacrifice, that keeps us from knowing true Peace, Love, and Unity.

If we're to successfully weather global pandemics, climate disasters, and societal mega-shifts, we need to turn our attention inward to our own self-discovery and awareness.

Imagine a world where each person lives in such a state of self-acceptance that they have no need or desire to prove their worth or superiority to anyone else. What might that world look and feel like?

To *be* human is to exist in a perpetual state of celebrating, elevating, and activating our glorious true Self. The place we must start is with discovering and loving our wholeness ***now***. The ***I am*** who is magical, congruent, connected, and personifies "perfect" by simply sitting still and **being**.

I witness myself daily now, learning to accept that the only thing I have control over is myself. I don't abdicate my commitment to ***right action***, nor do I condone violence, abuse, or bigotry in any form.

I simply no longer make my biggest impact in the world by burning myself out or living out of alignment just so my ego can feel validated.

The more I let go of trying, working hard, and pushing myself, the more I experience a greater state of inner peace.

I simply *am* because I *am*. I'm allowed to *be me*, as I *am*, and this is *enough*.

Here's what I've come to know since allowing my old identity of activist and political operative to die...

I still care deeply. I'm here to share my gifts and passion with the world for the elevation and evolution of all of us. My activist's heart hasn't gone anywhere; it's simply softened and shifted the way it understands its dharmic purpose.

The more I allow myself to rest, reboot, and recalibrate, the more I begin to show up in increasingly peaceful, loving, and connected ways that are more potent, aligned, and successful than before.

I'm no longer trying to "save the world." I'm simply allowing myself to live the most peaceful, loving, and connected life possible, and trusting that my greatest contributions flow from that.

This is what it truly means to "Be the change you wish to see in the world."
—Gandhi

Guiding Principles for Shifting the World

* Shift yourself first—all true change emanates from within.
* Beware of your assumption that the world needs shifting.
* We can only empower ourselves, no one else, and vice versa.
* We can only know our own Truth.
* Peace, Love, Unity, Abundance, and Joy exist within us and are therefore always available to us.
* Our greatest purpose is to constantly circulate these gifts throughout the universe.
* Dysfunctional and toxic systems of harm all are born from a wounded identity of Self.
* Our addiction to hurrying, chasing, pushing, and trying depletes our core resources and blocks true creativity and peace.

Questions to Challenge Old Paradigms

* Why are we always in such a **hurry—from** what, **to** what?
* How are the things that we're fighting against actually **alive in us**?
* How might we be **perpetuating** old paradigms and systems of harm through our unfelt emotions and incongruent actions and attitudes?
* How can we allow our **attachment** to our old identity to die without losing ourselves?
* What's our greatest **fear** about retiring old systems, paradigms, and patterns to live in alignment with our Truth?
* What can you start to **allow** in your life to generate more Peace, Love, and Unity?

Resources to Boost Your Expanding Consciousness & Compassion

***Kyle Cease**, *I Hope I Screw This Up*
https://kylecease.com/
***Lama Tsultrim Allione**, *Feeding Your Demons*
https://www.lionsroar.com/how-to-practice-feeding-your-demons/
***Mooji,** https://mooji.org/
***Nick Ortner,** The Tapping Solution
https://www.thetappingsolution.com/
***Pema Chödrön**, Maître Practice
https://www.youtube.com/watch?v=PRhkrQFbERs
***Ram Dass w/Jamie Cato**, "*Becoming Nobody*"
https://becomingnobody.com/
***Reverend Angel Kyodo Williams**, The Liberated Life Network
https://angelkyodowilliams.com/
***Saniel Bonder**, *Waking Down*
https://www.sanielandlinda.com/waking_down.html

Ariel Bickel

Ariel Bickel, visionary rebel, transformational leader, and international best-selling author, is the creator of *The Shifters Collective* and WOFILA (*Women Of Fire In a Life Aflame*) movements. Her paradigm-shifting philosophy and signature program, *Becoming the Fire*, is a dynamic catalyst for personal transformation and liberation. For three decades, Ariel has supported and activated thousands through her consulting, coaching, public speaking, writing, teaching, and community organizing. Ariel's intricate, unique perspective on the Shero's/Hero's Journey informs everything she does.

Abducted by her father twice before she turned five, successfully hidden from her mother, trained to lie about her true identity until eventually forgetting who she was, and raised in an environment of abuse, intimidation, and indoctrination until she left home at eighteen, Ariel intimately understands the pain and pleasure of setting off into the unknown to rediscover and reclaim your own Truth. She is a shameless advocate for people empowering themselves, and uses her own life wisdom to guide them in their awakening to their divine greatness.

With courage, tenacity, and vulnerability, Ariel guides people along their paths to self-discovery, inciting their desire to reclaim and redefine their power and purpose. Her ultimate goal is to instigate and accelerate the process of self-healing and transformation. With her wisdom and fierce compassion, she inspires others to live fully, freely, and unapologetically, and delights in the facilitation of raw, authentic self-expression and contribution. Her greatest pleasure is helping others to live, lead, and thrive from a place of rebellious joy and radical gratitude.

Email Address: **ariel@arielbickel.com**
Phone Number: 505-321-6867
Website: **arielbickel.com**
Facebook: **https://www.facebook.com/BEingArielBickel/**
LinkedIn: **https://www.linkedin.com/in/ariel-bickel-935aa07/**
Twitter: **@atbickel**
Instagram: **https://www.instagram.com/atbickel/**

LOVE ALL THE PIECES OF THE UNIVERSE
BY KARINA ARAGON

2020 was quite a year as predicted, a year of gestation and the dismantling of the old world. We've had to learn to communicate in new ways and navigate through the new world of technology and online commerce. This was a year of rearranging the parts that were already manifested in existence.

Openness

"What the world needs most is openness: open hearts, open doors, open eyes, open mind, open ears, and open souls."
—Robert Muller

Be open to abundance; the universe wants to bless you, but you must first allow it. Being in a state of receptivity and embracing the feminine energy within as this will assist you on your journey into receiving abundance. Be open to change, sometimes for our prayers to be answered or our dreams to come true; the universe will need to take things away and rearrange to make room for your gifts. We must let go of attachments, which include people, places, things, and even our attachments to the past and future. Practice living fully in the present, and you will start to feel the unconditional love of the universe. Yes, we have experienced a lot of loss—loss of a past identity, our jobs, livelihoods, some of us lost our homes, family members, and friends, and ultimately, we lost our vision.

Empathy

"You cannot do a kindness too soon, for you
never know when it will be too late."
—Ralph Waldo Emerson

We don't know a stranger's story or what someone might be going through in life. We could have a positive impact on someone that just lost a loved one or had plans later that day to commit suicide. Have compassion, as we are all fighting our own battles. We are adapting to the 2020 vision, the year in which this wild ride started, filled with radical shifts and what I call "the mass awakening." Awakening from what, you might ask? An awakening to what our true values are, where we come from, who we really are, and why we came here.

Third Eye

"I have three eyes: Two to look and One to see."
—Bellamor

Our third eye is an important part of awakening, and it is assisted by our pineal gland, which is located in our brain. The pineal gland produces melatonin, a serotonin-derived hormone that modulates sleep patterns in both circadian and seasonal cycles. This gland activates that connection we have to our higher self, also known as God. *The ancient philosophers believed that it is the seat of our soul. When it is activated and being utilized, it helps us see into the future, communicates with our intuition, makes sense of our potential, and assists us in identifying our underlying patterns in life.* Sounds pretty important, right? Did you know excess fluoride, chemicals, blue light, aluminum, and other heavy metals are linked to Alzheimer's? Research is plentiful, but just to name one, the US National Library of Medicine National Institutes of Health found specifically, fluoride is an acute toxin, with a rating slightly higher than lead. I encourage you to do your own research. Blue light naturally comes from the sun and is one of the light spectrums in our everyday electronic screens. Make sure to detox often, drink alkalized water, and get some blue light protection glasses when using your screens.

Network

"Teamwork makes the dream work."
—John C. Maxwell

Working with others, connecting with the community, and creating groups of like minds will help us level up and make bigger changes. Have you ever noticed networks are similar to spiderwebs? They are set up to feed our businesses and invite customers in. Spiders not only build a web for capturing their prey, but it's also used for relocating. For example, some spiders spin silk threads to catch the wind and then sail on the wind to a new location. Much like networking, it helps us gain our client base, put food on the table, and buy a house in the area we desire. Step up, be a leader, and start creating a team. If we think for a moment, prepare a plan, and delegate the right people to orchestrate the vision, we might have a chance at a beautiful new beginning. More leaders are needed to step up, share their voice, and unite communities that share a similar goal. I think humanity has come a long way, and I'm excited to see the evolution and the forward momentum.

Vitality

"Sometimes your whole life boils down to one insane move."
—Avatar

A flowing river never dies. The laws of physics found in Bernoulli's Principle states that as the speed of a moving fluid, liquid, or gas increases, the pressure within the fluid decreases. We are made up of all that, and if we keep our body moving, as in taking action toward our goals, the pressure inside will decrease, so if you're feeling stressed or under pressure, take action.

Experience

"Travel is fatal to prejudice, bigotry, and narrow-mindedness, and many of our people need it sorely on these accounts."
—Mark Twain

When we change our thoughts, we change our experiences. Your knowledge is based on experience, and it is said a bad experience is a lesson learned. We don't know until we experience something for ourselves. My best advice is to seek the experiences of other cultures, traditions, religions, and lands. Traveling is the best way to understand another. Every person is raised with different conditions, from what people eat, whom people marry, and how people pray. Be open to other ways of life; you might just learn something.

People also are increasingly caring about our children and how they are being treated as well as our animals. As a collective, we are awakening to the evil that the old system stood for as it fights tooth and nail to stay implemented. The old system has been dismantling as we create new systems as the evolution of the new world unfolds.

Embrace

"Embrace uncertainty. Some of the most beautiful chapters in our lives won't have titles until much later."
—Bob Goff

You never know why things happen or why life unexpectedly changes. Know that everything is in your best interest, even if you don't see the meaning yet. Embrace your good qualities and bad qualities, embrace the endings as well as the new beginnings, and embrace your journey. Everyone is on their personal journey, and comparing yourself will only frustrate you.

The systems society has known for so long are upgrading as well as our human DNA; **we are evolving into a new kind of human being.** As each human being upgrades, humanity as a whole is also upgrading.

Literally, the whole world had to shut down in order to start anew. The old world wasn't creating an awakened, purpose-driven, happy society anyway, right? So why did we want things to go back to "normal"? I want to live in a world that values unity.

Appreciation

"Be thankful for what you have; you'll end up having more. if you concentrate on what you don't have, you will never, ever have enough."
—Oprah Winfrey

Being in appreciation for what you have, the people in your life, and the things you are granted, the universe will continue pouring into our grateful cups.

Freedom is in the air; the chains are rusty and losing their grip. The old system sells fear, doubt to stay in control and enslave people blindly. **I**

believe the pandemic was the catalyst for change and reminded us that we are love, peace, and unity embodied. The screens hypnotize and ruin lives as it alters and twists the watcher's reality, opinions, and perception. The media shows us that the old system is trying to keep us bound by creating the illusion that we are the same kind of human as before. *The Neverending Story* quoted, "*If you can get someone to lose hope, you have won the control, and the one that has the control has the power.*" However, the 2020 system shutdown gave us time to breathe our own breath, no pun intended, and see the corrupt system for what it is. The old world mentality is to keep the little hands busy in order to keep the minds little. For the first time in our lives, we were told to be still to connect with the unconditional love energy within and pull out what is of value in our lives. It wasn't our jobs, necessarily, that we loved; it was what the jobs could supply for us.

We realized that we could have this without keeping the job we hate; we could do this by doing what we love by creating and unifying. We cannot be defeated if we stand as one unit, awaken to our unity consciousness as we continue to evolve into a new kind of human race. Saturn and Jupiter entered into Aquarius and conjunct at 0 degrees on December 21, 2020. My understanding of this conjunction marks the giving way to the new era and Age of Aquarius as we continue to see the dawning of the new world. Some people refer to it as the new Earth moving from the 3D consciousness into 5D consciousness, and I refer to it as the new world. There is a split being experienced in consciousness as each person has the freedom of choice.

"Just because you don't understand something
doesn't mean it's nonsense."
—Lemony Snicket

In my opinion, the old world is selling us separation. As seen on TV, like separation politically, blue versus red, racially, sexual orientation, social status, health status, country, borders, and walls. This is all under the umbrella of the 3D matrix and old world. The new world has a system of diversified power, not the hierarchy of power like the old world.

Understanding

"Seek to understand, not to be understood."
—Stephen Covey

We can all complain, judge, and condemn others for their differences, or we can accept with complete understanding and forgiveness that we are unique individuals that have had our own battles to overcome. ***With different eyes, we see different perspectives. We all have a story with an array of experiences that shape and mold our individual perspectives. Please open up and share your views, stories, and experiences with the world so we can better understand what you are made of; we are all listening and waiting to discover what makes you, well, you.***

Astrologically speaking, 2021 through 2023, our focus will be cultivating self-reliance in working with the natural world of our values and balancing that while exposing our truths through the transformation of our authentic experiences. The worldwide web is also undergoing a transformation. We are exiting an age of information and entering an age of value. Collectively, we are exiting the age of illusion (Pisces) and entering the age of radical revolution (Aquarius). The internet has been a beautiful thing for so long, giving us plentiful amounts of uncensored information. This is what I refer to as the age of information. We are now moving into the age of value, which is sorting through what is valuable information. Now that we are entering the new world let's not repeat history as before. The revolutionaries not only destroyed the old ties but were unable to establish the kind of new ties they would have liked; they wound up with a very different society from the one they anticipated. With that being said, we are in the year of building a new foundation for the new world. Let's do it right this time, so we don't repeat history and fail to create the kind of new world we are envisioning.

We are to be focused on building our new system based on our new values. We're slowly implementing our new values within our systems, including our schools, governments, currency, and our own personal lives.

What does humanity want to create next? Do we want to build a value system based on family, unity, oneness, equality, and helping others? Do we want to create healthy alternatives for our earth? We're not going to be able to sustain the old world of consumerism, greed, power, hate, and pollution. We have to make a choice; to be or not to be, that is the question.

Cultivation

"We must cultivate our own garden."
—Voltaire

Remember, your current situation is not your final destination; the best is yet to come. The key is to cultivate compassion and understanding that we are all different. We have different strengths and weaknesses. Your failures may be someone else's successes and vice versa.

If we knew where a person came from, what it took for them to get where they are, we would be more compassionate and less envious. Celebrate the wins; regardless if it's big or small, they both need attention. Remember, it's the little things and the daily baby steps that get us the big successful outcomes.

Unity consciousness was an unknown term not too long ago. Now, it's a worldwide word with substance and meaning, "we are all one," and we know exactly what that means. We see more people caring about others besides their own race, religion, country, and background. We are seeing these positive movements like "Me Too" and "Black Lives Matter," uniting as one against prejudices, unfair acts, and unlawful crimes. Make sure that you understand the difference between supporting and segregation.

PATIENCE

"Visualize, exercise, and trust in the process."
—Karina Aragon

Know that everyone is on their own timeline and pace. Things expand and contract just as the planet Saturn brings blessings of hard work and diligence; Jupiter brings blessings of luck and chance. Everyone will have their moment, including you, so stay steady and hopeful for when the planets spin into your field. Start off with a purpose-filled vision while creating opportunities, and allow the universe to do the rest.

The truth is the old system of control and the 3D matrix will not survive. Our universe ultimately has the power. Did you know the earth's magnetic field and sun's magnetic poles shift and flip polarity? The sun flips polarity approximately every eleven years; the last flip was 2012–2013. I personally think it will flip earlier than later. Also, the earth flips its polarity approximately every 200k to 300k years; evidence shows it has been approximately 780k years since the last polarity flip, and yes, you guessed it, the earth is overdue. Much of this information could be found on the following websites, NASA, Earthsky, and National Geographic. The meters as of recent years show the magnetic north pole is shifting approximately thirty miles every year. When the earth decides to totally flip its polarity, we will experience many earthly shifts. Our compasses will show north when facing south and south when facing north. This will have harmful effects on our migratory animals; birdlife and mass extinction in some species will occur. Our mother Gaia will shift with the rest of us, creating more earthquakes, tsunamis, and weather shifts. Humanity also will have some disruptions with the one thing we've relied on, our satellites, the internet, and cell phones. Some of the new world technology dependency may be jeopardized, so with that being said, let's negate its impact by working together as one to find solutions to these substantial future shifts.

Integration

"God does not care about our mathematical difficulties. He integrates empirically."
—Albert Einstein

There are so many more shifts, changes, and new energies ahead that we are being asked by the universe to practice integration. Integration of mind, body, spirit, integration of humanity, and the integration of all the new radiation flying through our solar system. Our beliefs create our reality, so make it a point to believe that which you want to manifest. Our health depends on our belief in the intelligence of our bodies.

You

"Should I be the one to play God? We are both about the same age, but we grew up in different neighborhoods."
—George Burns

Everything always starts with you. Do you know who you are? You are a part of this universe and everyone in it. We are all connected to the divine spirit of the universe, and we are the creators. We create everything in 3D as we manifest in the 5D. Per the law of physics and *the law of conservation of energy, energy can neither be created nor destroyed, but it can be transformed from one form to another. Since energy cannot be created or destroyed, the amount of energy present in the universe always remains constant.* With that being said, our soul and spirit never die, we return to the cosmos, and the cycle starts again. I believe our souls are recycled when we are not bound to our bodies and flow through the universe, transforming and transferring somewhere else. Our bodies as well are recycled, as our decomposed remains feed the trees and remaining life. *Remember, never worry about lack; the lack mentality will only bring you more lack, and lack is an illusion in this 3D matrix.* We always have everything we need; the universe is wise, loving, and abundant.

Humanity is undergoing a system reboot, and our job is to keep moving forward, keep a positive outlook, enjoy the roller coaster, and keep smiling.

Laughter

"Against the assault of laughter, nothing can stand."
—Mark Twain

A few things I learned in my studies in psychology is the magic dynamics of the brain. Laugh often; the act of smiling and laughing creates endorphins. Yes, you heard correctly, when you smile, your brain releases tiny molecules called neuropeptides to help fight off stress. According to neuropsychology, there are other neurotransmitters like dopamine, serotonin, and endorphins that are activated and act as a mild pain reliever, whereas serotonin is an antidepressant, so it's all good with a laugh.

Key Break Free for Humanity Quotes

PEACE

Patience
"Visualize, exercise, and trust the process." —Karina Aragon

Empathy
"You cannot do a kindness too soon, for you never know when it will be too late." —Ralph Waldo Emerson

Appreciation
"Be thankful for what you have; you'll end up having more. if you concentrate on what you don't have, you will never, ever have enough." —Oprah Winfrey

Cultivation
"We must cultivate our own garden." —Voltaire

"Remember, your current situation is not your final destination. The best is yet to come." —Zig Ziglar

Experience
"Travel is fatal to prejudice, bigotry, and narrow-mindedness, and many of our people need it sorely on these accounts." —Mark Twain

LOVE

Laughter
"Against the assault of laughter, nothing can stand." —Mark Twain

Openness
"What the world needs most is Openness: open hearts, open doors, open eyes, open mind, open ears, and open souls." —Robert Muller

Vitality
"Sometimes your whole life boils down to one insane move." —Avatar

Embrace
"Embrace uncertainty. Some of the most beautiful chapters in our lives won't have titles until much later." —Bob Goff

UNITY

Understanding
"Just because you don't understand something doesn't mean it's nonsense." —Lemony Snicket

Network
"Teamwork makes the dream work."

Integrity
"If you tell the truth, you don't have to remember anything." —Mark Twain

Tolerance
"Inner compassion and outer tolerance can easily make a new world, a better world." —Sri Chinmoy

You
"Should I be the one to play God? We are both about the same age, but we grew up in different neighborhoods." —George Burns

We are all one in the universe; unity underlying diversity in love, peace, and unity as we create the new world.

Karina Aragon

Karina is an entrepreneur, Intuitive Transformational Coach at Lucid Living Movement, and an international bestselling author of *Break Free to Stand in Your Power*. She loves to inspire, create, and heal. She has been an entrepreneur for over twelve years, creating CK Cleanliving, a successful cleaning and organizing business.

Karina desires to assist the collective through the transformation into building the new world. She wants to make a difference in the communities around the world through inspirational speaking, healing arts, and teaching practical astrology. She is an intuitive transformational coach, astrologist, card reader, and art therapist.

She uses a three-step process when coaching her clients. First, she pulls the astrological birth chart, which assesses the galactic cosmos to get acquainted with her client's "soul DNA," which accelerates the healing and coaching process. The second step consists of talk therapy to assist in identifying any root issues that may be getting in the way of her client's goals. Lastly, she works with them to develop goals, mapping out a plan of accomplishment to reach those goals, and be on their soul's divine purpose.

"Let's evolve and heal the collective one person at a time. We may not be able to reach everyone all at once, but if we make a difference in one person's life and our direct communities, we will expand and make changes on a bigger scale."

Phone: 510-691-3611
Email: **LucidLivingLeoQueen@gmail.com**
Website: **www.LucidLivingMovement.com**
Facebook: **https://www.facebook.com/LucidLivingMovement/**
Instagram: **https://www.instagram.com/lucid_living_coach/**
Twitter: **https://twitter.com/KLA_LucidLiving**
YouTube: **http://www.youtube.com/c/KarinaAragonYourLucidLivingCoach**
WordPress: **https://wordpress.com/view/lucidlivingmovement.wordpress.com**

Part 2: Discover Your Greatness

IN SPITE OF ALL ODDS
BY NISCHAL GOSWAMI

I truly believe life is what you make it. If a small girl running through the shore of the Ganges, the holy river of India, eating wild berries picked straight from the trees, and sitting hours on the stairs of the temple can one day be working with hundreds of trained professionals and then training them, then I know life is what you make it, as I was once that little girl.

In the left corner of the courtyard of my house, my grandmother used to sit wearing a white saree and having her hair done; she used to talk to me about great women who served the nation, those people who never stopped themselves because of what other people said. All those words left powerful seeds in my mind. Growing up in a small town, having people close to me, who love you as you are, has been a blessing for me. I have a big brother and a sister, and I was the youngest of the lot; my father was a politician and a teacher and the greatest man I have ever come across in my life. He used to always say, "Truthfulness is the key to success." My mother, though a housewife, was my first mentor. She gave me detailed life lessons and had a solution for everything. It was as if she had lived the same life! But in reality, her whole life revolved around us. She was the reason for the unity the house had. We were all different; we had different attitudes and different mindsets, but we were all connected not because we were a family and had the same blood but because we accepted each other for who we were as people. When I grew older and went to college and met other people, I felt the same warmth as I felt in my home. **All those years of my grandmother's stories and my mother's advice worked well for me. I was not afraid of the unknown, and I was ready for every challenge ahead in my life.**

I got married when I was twenty to a very handsome, bright man—the true definition of tall, dark, and handsome. I truly believe I got lucky in this area, and so did he! As partners, we never let the communication break. We knew each other well, and that helped us to overcome every obstacle together as a team. Sometimes it was him leading, and sometimes it was me leading the situation. The very basis of a relationship is trust and respect, and we both had a lot of trust and respect for each other. We complemented each other, and we worked as a team. A very important bridge in our relationship was my mother-in-law; she was a beauty personified. A true example of a strong woman who taught me how to take control of my life and how to respect every individual in the family. Coming from a village and not knowing how to read and write, she raised six sons who are well established now. It was because of her that I decided to take my children to the next level. And that led me to open new doors, and I welcomed every opportunity that came my way.

I knew from the very beginning that I am not the person who gives up, even if I do not know how to do a certain thing. I never worked, even in my mother's house, and when I got married, I had to take care of the house because I was the lady of the house, and before I realized it, I was working for an IT company. There I was, looking at the screen of the computer and not knowing what to do next. On that very day, I felt uncomfortable. I felt like running away and just going back home to my kids. But I reminded myself of what my mother taught me. She said, "You fix a goal, and you aim for it and push away the other obstacles." I sat back in the chair and started working.

Later, I shifted to another company and started a new domain of work; this opportunity in my life was the beginning of a whole new life. Seema Giri was my next mentor, and I found another sister and a best friend. She came from the United States, and so did her husband, Upendra, who is my brother-in-law, and we started a new venture. It was a whole new domain for me, and if it were not for Seema, I wouldn't have realized how capable I am. There were rough times too, but I always knew that I have a woman who is strong as a rock always beside me. Slowly and gradually, things started to settle down, and after some time, I was designated as the HR director. My priority were my kids. I started working for them and soon found myself, too. Seema and I always used to laugh about how extremely different we were, and sometimes, we used to have deep conversations. She was and still is my best friend. As time passed, I explored new opportunities, which deepened the connection to my authentic self, and I was living the life I was meant to live. **A single person can never achieve anything alone; it was the collective love and a spirit of oneness that led me to become who I am.** I learned a new thing every day during work. I never bounded myself to the things people told me about my limitations. I always felt that I could do anything. I always followed a simple logic: if someone has already done it, it is doable; and if no one has done it, be the first one to experiment. I found peace when I worked, and I saw my team as my family, and we treated each other as family.

A life lived with smoothness is half a life, and I have a tendency to do everything in the extreme. I was diagnosed with breast cancer in 2014; it came as a shock to the whole family and the company. I was unaware of what was going to happen next, and the question was am I going to live or not. I decided to fight. I knew it was going to be tough, but I also knew that I was tougher. I had cycles of chemo and radiation, and I recovered from breast cancer. All this time, the one thing that helped me go through

all this was my family. I was motivated from the oldest to the youngest person in my family. I was bald, and I was beautiful, and that time, I realized that it is not your physical beauty that matters; people who love you because of who you are on the inside. Everyone stood rock solid like a team. My in-laws were my support system; they treated me like nothing was wrong and never let me know when things were not going in my favor, and maybe this is the reason why things didn't go wrong. **After I recovered, I bounced back. I started working again. All this time, I taught my children some valuable lessons, but I did not know they had to learn more.** After exactly four years, I was diagnosed with fourth stage bone cancer. **This time, I thought things were not going my way, and the end was near. It was not death I feared; it was the feeling of not doing enough, the feeling that I can do better than before, and now I am being stopped.** We slowly revealed to the other family members and then my children. This time, they were older; they knew what was happening, and they stood right in front of me and said, "We will face it together, and not even God can take you." We were all in this together. **And this time, we knew what the process was. I am still fighting, and I know I will fight until the cancer gives up.**

Throughout my life, I lived very courageously, and this courage has become a habit, and this habit will not be destroyed. **I always wondered if I was teaching my children the basic value of courage. I do not know if I did, but the situation did. And I feel proud when I see them. This brings me peace. My thoughts are straight, aligned with each other, and after all the events in my life, I can say that I am limitless. I am still learning, and I will never give up.**

People limit themselves, even when no one has told them, but because they think that they can do only this. I am saying you are limitless; you just have to trust yourself.

From the very beginning of my life, I have had powerful women energy with me: my grandmother taught me how you could change people's lives, my mother taught me whatever happens, you never leave your aim unaccomplished, my mother-in-law taught me how to be fierce and kind at the same time, my sister-in-law Seema taught me how a woman could do everything on her own, and my daughter who taught me that I could make a change in the world by just telling my story. These ladies helped me in my every endeavor. **As I look back, I know my journey has not been a fairytale, but who needs a fairytale when you have your own version of paradise? Life is what you make it; grab every opportunity, and treat it with love and patience.**

Who would have thought that a girl from a small town would be writing this? Take charge and grab every opportunity you encounter. Remember, you are limitless.

In Loving Memory of Nischal Goswami

Nischal Goswami was a human resource professional, cancer fighter, loving wife, and extraordinary mother. She had a superpower for connecting deeply with people and bringing out the very best in them, even talent and potential they didn't know they possessed.

Although she came from Allahabad, a small town in India, Nischal persevered to accomplish her goals of career, family, and community service. She was a symbol of courage, patience, and love. Although she ultimately succumbed to her battle with bone cancer, before she died, she chose to share her story here. Hopefully, it inspires others to do what is in their power to overcome their challenges.

RAISE YOUR FREQUENCY; CHANGE YOUR LIFE
BY SHARON CAREN

As a young girl, I loved going to church with my friends. There were many different places of worship; some were darker with stained glass windows and statues, others more modern-looking with slanted roofs and bright open windows, and I found it fascinating. Some had organ music and singing and sermons, reading scripture. I really connected with the different rituals. I felt warm deep within me and grateful for my friends taking me along.

Maybe I starved for love and nurturing. My parents did the best they could, but my mom, Lutheran, and my dad, Jewish, didn't agree on anything. There was no religion in our home. **I was eleven when my dad walked out on my younger sister, my mom, and me. It was hard; my mom and little sister were devastated. The best thing was the fighting stopped, and my inner curiosity strengthened and took over.**

During adolescence, Mom and I read the daily horoscope together. It was fascinating how each of us had different personalities according to our date of birth. This helped to explain why people had different ways of being. At night, I would gaze up at the stars and dream about the constellations and what was really going on out there.

At nineteen, I married my high school sweetheart (Steve). This was at the height of the Vietnam war. Steve was drafted and shipped out to serve during the Tet Offensive. I was afraid he would not return. I prayed he would survive working as a helicopter crew chief, rescuing wounded and dead bodies, and thankfully he did return. **However, he developed PTSD; we divorced after five years. As I recall, it brought back my deep childhood feelings of abandonment. I cried for the next three years.** I discovered during that time, everyone is always doing the best they can with what they have at any given moment.

Then at twenty-seven, I was ready to move on to a happy life with loving relationships. I began dating, met a nice guy, and went to a party with friends to find my newfound boyfriend with another woman. **It was more than I could bear, and I told my friends, "I'm out of here," driving off, devastated.** I drove down the freeway in the slow lane toward home and must've fallen asleep exhausted from working two jobs. My car spun out, and I hit the center divider going in the opposite direction. On impact with no seatbelt, my chest hit the passenger seat, and my head went down on the floorboard. **As I started to rise up, I found myself floating up and out of the car. This was it. While looking down, I saw my physical body gasping, and I was pulled back into my body. I wasn't done yet.**

Making another U-turn on the freeway, I drove my car home on two flat tires, and my neighbor drove me to St. Rose Emergency. It took five hours for x-rays when the intern on duty sent me home with bruises and said I'd be okay in a couple of days.

The next morning, I got a call from the hospital telling me I had to come back. I'd been vomiting from shock and got a ride back to the hospital. As I walked through the automatic doors at the hospital entry, they laid me flat on a stretcher with sandbags so I couldn't move my head and left me all alone in a dark room.

Dr. McGuire told me I had broken my neck. "You must be kidding? I drove my car home, walked all around, and then back to the hospital on my own accord. People who break their necks are dead," I said. He agreed; for many, it was true, but I was very much alive. All this was surreal, like a bad dream. It was a six-day struggle for life as I laid in traction completely drugged while Dr. McGuire tried with all he had to realign the vertebrae in my neck. On day 6, using a fifty-pound weight to pull apart and re-align the vertebrae, he then wrapped me in a fiberglass body cast while my neck healed naturally.

Hindsight is 20/20. I had many warning signals and didn't listen. I later learned it's the connection from the non-physical of body, mind, and spirit trying to get my attention. My Creator, angels, and spirit guides worked overtime to save me. The fifty-pound weight did the trick *this time.* The doctor warned if the bones didn't grow together and mend, I would still need a neck fusion. I *listened*, promising my Creator and myself I would continue listening from this day forward. Again, friends took me to church, I prayed, and I pictured the bones in my neck growing back together, visualizing every day, and that's exactly what I created. **Through this experience, I was then surrounded by wonderful new friends, light beings I met who were angels showing me divine loving compassion as I'd never experienced. When others hear that I broke my neck, the response is, "How terrible," and my response is, "No, it's the best thing that could have happened to me. I am blessed to be alive today. This was my wake-up call."**

We all have situations and circumstances, and they don't have us when we learn to connect with a higher power. What gives my life meaning is helping others realize that each one of us is made up of divine fragments of the Creator's light. I say, "the Creator source is in me and runs my being." **It's important to understand the dynamics of the energetic light force to grasp how connected we are and connected to all that is. I'll share what I've learned to assist you in your soul connection.**

Through your unique being, you project all aspects of this energy light source out into the world to illuminate the darkness. As you explore, grow, and expand, your energetic frequency rises, and the brighter your light becomes. This is called evolution. **You are an ever-evolving being of light having a human experience in an earth suit.**

Everything has an energetic frequency that's alive and always moving. Everything sparks from the frequency of light and has a unique vibration. You may have heard the term light beings and dark beings. This term speaks directly to a frequency vibration without judgement. When a thing comes into being, it has sparked from that light frequency. Nothing can spark from nothing, and dark energy is a very low, slow frequency. Dark just means "void of light." As something is created and comes into being, it sparks from a high frequency of light energy.

You are connected to everything because you live in an ocean of energy where everything is connected at the lowest terms in the unified field. So why might your soul want to incarnate on Earth when life may be so hard? It's to manifest into the physical world the aspects of the Creator source, to bring into form all the wondrous aspects of the Creator and live a life that uplifts your soul and those around you, also to evolve, reaching a higher frequency on your soul journey to evolution. Life seeks more life and is ever-expanding.

Coming to Earth is like taking a crash course. You've come in to experience and balance four bodies all at the same time: spiritual, physical, emotional, and mental.

View your body as part of a vast universe where soul, matter, and energy intersects. We are born with bioelectric "circuitry" called Chakras, a Sanskrit word that means "wheel." There are seven energy centers where the lifeforce (called *chi* in China or *prana* in India) flows through the body to restore and cleanse. This is meant to be a free-flowing system. If the energy flow is interrupted, the physical body cannot function with ease, and this will create dis-ease. Life traumas, giving away power to authority figures, or perceived fears can create a blockage in the Chakra system.

As I shared my story earlier, you can see how my energy source became blocked from childhood, marriage, and the trauma of a broken neck accident, so I could wake up and decide to make different choices. **So notice what you are noticing. I began to notice, looking back over my life, it was time to decide what I would love, knowing I am a creator. There is so much more to life than situations and circumstances!**

The spirit body, or etheric body, works in the non-physical and is connected to the infinite. The physical body connects to the energy body through the physical nervous system. It's our body's electrical system, and the spirit body breathes life energy into it through each of the Chakras.

I love working with clients to embrace this energy system to attain connectedness and divinity. To better understand Chakras and the role they play, we look to the East. In Eastern cultures, they maintain overall good health by understanding how the Chakras (energy centers) and the four bodies (spiritual, physical, emotional, mental) are connected and how this may affect everyday life.

The three lower Chakras connect us to the planet earth, also referred to as Gia, the earth mother. The upper three Chakras are spiritual and connect us to the spirit world, the creator source, God. Begin to notice how totally connected we are to all that is. The fourth Chakra, or heart Chakra, is in the middle, acting as a connector for the lower three with the upper three through the heart center. The heart Chakra gives balance while on Earth and connects us to spirit, the infinite part of ourselves. It's a beautifully designed system to assist in living a life we love. We have the opportunity for transformation and evolution, realizing there is so much more than what our five senses tell us!

Our planet was created in love and light. Our heart opens to let us know we are on track while embracing the inner power and connection with all that is.

For more information on Chakras, go to www.sharoncaren.com or https://bit.ly/sharoncaren for your free downloadable Chakra worksheet guide.

It's my understanding divine love and peace is the highest frequency we can attain here on Earth in a body. This is the divine love frequency of Mother Teresa and The Dalai Lama. These two beings have come to walk the Earth to show us what it looks like to become enlightened. Divine love is very different from caretaking love, which is conditionally based. Many of us learned only caretaking love from our childhood with a much lower frequency.

"Love moves through me, and I bring that love to others." **Remember, you are powerful beyond measure. You've got what it takes. You will get through this. Only you can bring your special gifts to the world. The content of your life is the curriculum of your evolution. The connection to your infinite nature will always seek more life. This is the energy that keeps you living, growing, and loving! (To quote Mary Morrissey, spiritual leader and bestselling author.)**

Now, let's look at the emotional body, where there are only two emotions. One is love, and one is fear. Love is expansive, and fear is contractive. To live a full and healthy life, make it a practice to notice what you're feeling. If you feel contractive, you are in fear energy. So begin by taking a deep breath into your belly, slowly through your nose, and exhale even slower through your mouth like you are blowing through a straw. Do this three to five times (or more) until you feel your nervous system slow down and feel your shoulders and forehead soften. This breathing method tells the physical body *you are safe.*

Let your breath continue from your lungs, down into your thighs and calf muscles, past the ankles, and into the bottom of your feet. While focusing on your breath, you may feel the tingling of your feet flat on the floor. This is your connection with Gia, the earth mother. You always have your breath with you, so use this technique whenever you feel fearful, anxious, or contractive. **Remember to *breathe*. You are safe and always connected.**

Your soul is always with you. It's who you are now and when you are not in a physical body. It's your life in-between lives in the spirit world in another dimension. You're a luminous light being having a human experience on the planet in an earth suit. You didn't create your body, and you don't even breathe yourself. **There is something far greater going on than what your five senses can detect. Call it God, Creator of all beings, higher self, universal Creator source, or whatever. I realized and embodied this concept after my broken neck.**

Okay, Earth is the hard place. It's not for sissies. The fact that you are here now means you are a powerful light being attending Earth school to learn from these difficult life experiences. You chose to be here during this tremendous time of change, to hold the light frequency and be part of the solution, bringing balance to the planet. My understanding is that one life on Earth is equal to many lifetimes in other places in the universe. We are on the fast track to evolve because Earth is where the rubber meets the road!

Power vs. Force, written by Dr. David R. Hawkins, is one of the many books he authored introducing the Map of Consciousness. As a nationally renowned psychiatrist, physician, researcher, spiritual teacher, and lecturer, his unique contribution to humanity comes from his enlightenment and self-realization. What a gift it is to see a physician and scientist attain this level of spiritual awareness. The Map of Consciousness tool was a game-changer for me. I share it with you so you may better understand energy. It's important to your physical body to create good health. I use this tool with my clients and personally as an energetic measuring guide.

Another great tool; learning to use a pendulum. Here you begin connecting to your intuition. It's the best way I've found to trust my gut and feel affirmed. You may have a feeling deep inside and know something even though it's not conscious. Trust it! If you feel adventurous, I recommend exploring the pendulum.

In the unified field, everything is connected, and all the information for all time is there for you to access. You are a powerful light being, and using this tool, you'll begin to realize what that means. Stay open to the possibilities and enjoy the ride as you develop and trust yourself.

Remember, this work is sacred. You'll become a clear vessel, curious to find meaningful answers for yourself and others without attachment to the outcome.

When you choose a pendulum, pay attention to how you feel. Look at and try different ones. Pendulums come in many different materials. Gemstones and crystals are beautiful and a bit lighter and bouncy when in use. There are different metals used, such as brass, that tend to be heavier, moving slower and smoothly. See what speaks to you. Is there a color or shape that catches your eye? Choose different ones for different uses and trade off. There's no right or wrong way, as your pendulum is very personal. Let go and trust the process. The perfect one will show up for you! Some people use a necklace chain with a weighted object at the end that swings freely back and forth under the influence of gravity. Whatever you use, make sure it feels really good to you.

This divination tool becomes an extension of you. Keep it close, in your pocket, and under your pillow at night. You'll become best friends and work well together. As children, we began learning from birth, and everything in the world was new. Go back to the childlike wonder and curiosity. Play and learn as you go, having fun without attachment to the outcome.

As you relax, breathe into your heart space (the love energy) and practice being in a neutral space. This is a relaxed type of altered state. It's not meditation as you are aware of your surroundings. It's a place of exploration and curiosity while you ask yes-and-no questions. You'll begin to trust your intuitive nature. This is a way for you to tap into the all-knowing part of yourself that has all the answers. It's the connection with your infinite nature and where your power is. The movement of the pendulum works through your body's nervous system and the galvanic skin response, bringing forth the information for the highest good of all. Be open, and you'll learn to master your new tool. (Go to www.sharoncaren.com or https://bit.ly/sharoncaren if you have an interest in my online pendulum course.)

What I've shared here is spiritually universal. As you explore and expand, you discover that you really do have all the answers and will trust yourself, a beautiful light being that has come to share your unique gifts with the world. I'm here to support you all the way!

Takeaway Tips:

1. Breathe deeply into your belly and down into the Earth.

2. Ground. Feel your connection with the Earth. You are safe.

3. Remember, you have unique gifts to bring to the world.

"Your sacred space is where you can find yourself over and over again." (Joseph Campbell)

Sharon Caren

As a spiritual intuitive speaker and transformational coach, Sharon guides women struggling with the death of a spouse or child, divorce, career changes, retirement, and empty-nesters to find their deep soul connection and life purpose. Their lives forever change and open to a fuller and more powerful expression.

After her lifetime of knowledge in healing and personal awakening, Sharon has mastered serving clients' connection with the infinite. Through her programs in the akashic field, she provides readings/healings, spiritual coaching, and classes to support soul evolution. She loves speaking to groups and also teaching a complete training certification in the akashic system to leave her legacy. For those who are ready to step into purpose and power, this work will assist in the evolution of humanity in these ever-changing times.

"Sharon's Akashic Training is the best out there with the level of detail, explanation, content, and support. You'll build a thriving business whether you're a novice or want to add to your healing practice based on what you learn in her program. I highly recommend Sharon to anyone wanting to go deeper in their own spiritual work and to help more people." (Lauren Brollier, founder of Soul Savvy)

Sharon, her husband Dave, and five-pound chihuahua, Little Charlie, live on the beautiful California coast in the San Francisco Bay area. They love taking walks on the beach, old-time rock n' roll music (Dave's a musician), and sharing time with family and friends.

www.sharoncaren.com
sharon@sharoncaren.com
Cell/text 650.922.7951
https://www.facebook.com/SharonsUniqueSpirit
https://www.instagram.com/SharonsUniqueSpirit
https://twitter.com/sharoncaren
https://www.linkedin.com/in/sharoncaren
https://www.youtube.com/user/sharoncaren

YOU ARE LOVED
BY DEBBIE CAMPBELL

Maria Cabibi was born in a small Sicilian town. There wasn't much work, so in 1911, her father, Fillipo, set off to America. Fillipo went alone to find work and ended up working in the mines of Colorado.

In 1913, Maria, her siblings, and her mother, Paolo, set out to join her father in America. They had to ride in a wagon to the big port city of Palermo. Many ships were sailing to America, but for poor peasants, the only choice was to sail in steerage.

The voyage took three months, and when they arrived at Ellis Island, New York, they were filth, hungry, and lice-ridden. There were so many immigrants, and the family felt even more like cattle being herded about. Maria's long hair was cut off, and they were cleaned up. The family had to ride a train to Pueblo, Colorado, to reunite with Fillipo.

At nine years old, Maria was the oldest child in her family. It was hard to be in a new place with a strange language. The family sent Maria to school, but since she had no formal education and did not know English, she was put in a class with kindergarten students. Being so much older was humiliating, and she struggled to learn the language.

Maria eventually learned English fairly well and continued through third grade. She also adopted the name "Marie" to be more American. At that point, there were more young siblings at home, and her mother needed her help. The third grade was all the education she ever completed.

When Marie was in her twenties, she was sent out to California to help some relatives with their small children. The Sicilian community was large in San Jose, and at some point, she met her husband-to-be, Domenic Geraci.

Marie raised three children, two boys and a girl, and also worked seasonally at a cannery. Domenic was a foreman at the tomato cannery. Domenic had a green thumb and could grow anything. After they saved some money, Domenic bought ten acres of apricot orchards in the Central Valley of California.

Marie Cabibi Geraci was my grandmother and the greatest influence in my life. By the time I was five years old, my parents had divorced, and my mom was on her own. My grandparents lived close by and often watched my younger brother and me. **My grandparents lived in the same house that my grandfather was raised in. My mom still lives there today. I always felt at home there and that I would always have a home to go to. The family home was the one stability in my life.**

My mom worked nights in the canneries and factories, so I spent a lot of time with my grandmother. **Marie was kind and giving, and that spirit has been passed down to me.** It was normal to offer friends food and help (especially food!).

Marie crocheted beautifully, but never from a pattern. I learned to crochet from her (although never as well), and I would roll up the balls of yarn for her. **My grandmother was not a big talker and seemed quiet. She was always teaching me things, and some of my favorite times with her were baking Sicilian cookies from old family recipes.**

My grandfather was quite the opposite. He had a busted eardrum in one ear and could not hear well. Between that and working in a loud environment, he spoke loudly and always seemed like he was yelling. I know he loved me, but as a young child, he was kind of intimidating. I knew I always had my grandmother on my side, though, and I felt protected by her.

My mom had to work very hard, and I know that there were times we would barely scrape by. I now know that we probably would not have had food if not for my grandmother. An Italian mom will always make sure everybody gets fed!

My summers were spent with my grandparents at their apricot orchards since my mom worked a lot at that time of year. I worked every summer riding the tractor, putting out boxes, and picking the fruit when it was ripe. We would cut apricots, and my grandfather had a sulfur shed for drying them. It was hard work, but I feel blessed to have had the chance to live in both the city and the country. Hard work was expected of everyone.

Summers were my favorite time. I loved the country and even the hard work. My grandmother taught me how to play Canasta and feed chickens. She cleaned fish (which I learned, but don't enjoy) and even had to kill a mean rooster one time (which I have never done!). She was so strong and resilient. My grandfather was the man of the house, but I somehow knew that Marie was the one in charge.

Growing up without a father was hard and not that common at the time. I was insecure as a young girl and I found solace in school. I did very well in school, and I loved it. School was the one place I felt like I belonged. My school was in a lower-middle-class area, and we did not even have a library. **I was fortunate to have the most exceptional teachers, though, and found books to be inspiring.**

Since I was the oldest child, there were a lot of expectations and pressures put on me. I had to help with my brother, and I learned to be responsible at an early age, although, at times, I resented it.

I never felt that I was good enough. I normally got straight-As on my report cards, but if I got an A-minus or a B-plus, my grandfather or mother would ask me why I did not get an A. My friends would take sewing or home economics, and my mom would ask me why I didn't do that, too. No matter what I did or how well I performed, I was expected to do more or be better. This feeling stuck with me for most of my life. I felt like you had to earn love.

The only person that would accept me as I am was my grandmother. I always felt her love and kindness. She would encourage me and never criticized me at all. Even at my worst (and there were plenty of those times), I knew I could be myself, and she would love me no matter what. An unconditional love, with no strings attached, is an amazing thing.

My life went through many twists and turns, but my grandmother always forgave me for my mistakes and loved me through good times and bad. By the time I had kids of my own, my grandmother was frailer but still had the gentle strength she always had. I have a picture that I love of four generations of women, from my grandmother to my daughter. My grandmother is in a wheelchair, holding my daughter. The love in her eyes is astounding and makes me happy to this day.

I had to work on my self-esteem over the years, and I wanted my own children to feel safe and loved, always. I can thank my grandmother for showing me how to do that. I tried to show my children that I would always love them, no matter what. I wanted them to be kind,

caring, and yet strong. I never wanted them to feel like love has strings attached as I did.

My grandmother ended up in a nursing home after breaking her hip. My grandfather got sick during this time and passed away. I remember taking my grandmother to the funeral and even though she looked weak, I could see her strength.

My family and I visited her every week after church. I could see she was declining by this point. My uncle, her middle son, had a heart attack and had to have emergency bypass surgery. We found out later that right after my uncle came out of surgery and was doing okay was when my grandmother passed away. I feel like she was waiting to make sure her family was okay before she could leave. It was almost six months to the day that her husband had passed. I am sure my grandfather was waiting for her to join him.

My grandmother's funeral was more subdued than my grandfather's had been. It was raining, my one uncle was in the hospital, and fewer people attended. I know the family doesn't always talk at the service, but since no one else stood up, I decided I needed to speak. She deserved that much.

I told everyone that while my grandmother was quiet, she was the strong glue that held our family together. The women in my family are strong because they had to be. I am proud to be a strong woman, too.

I hope that you have someone in your life that encourages you and loves you unconditionally. If you don't, please don't despair, as I'm sure you will eventually. I searched for a long time to find that love in my own life, but because of Marie Cabibi Geraci, I knew it did exist.

Surround yourself with loving and kind people, and **know that you *are* good enough and deserve to be loved.** This is what I would go back and remind myself of during all the hard parts of my life.

We all have struggles in life and feel hopeless at times. **Don't hesitate to ask for help, and don't be afraid to be loved and cared for. Share your own love with the world around you. Love is meant to be shared and expanded. You are exceptional and, above all, *loved*.**

Debbie Campbell

Debbie Campbell was born and raised in San Jose, California. She has also lived in Florida, North Carolina and Connecticut, and enjoyed a 16-year stint in Ohio. The midwest is a great place to raise a family, but Debbie is a California girl at heart. Debbie has been published in the *Marina Gazette*, but *Break Free to Peace, Love & Unity* is her first book.

Debbie has a full-time job in global supply chain planning and a Touchstone Crystal by Swarovski business. Debbie has two adult children, and lives with her husband, Ray, and cocker spaniel, Louie, on the beautiful central coast of California.

Facebook: **https://www.facebook.com/deb.touchstonecrystal**
Instagram: **https://www.instagram.com/debcsparkle/**
Twitter: **https://twitter.com/Debknowsbest1**

FAIL FORWARD
YOU CAN BE ANYTHING YOU CHOOSE TO BE
BY SUNIL CHERIAN

In our culture, we are conditioned to always be perfect, and to avoid making mistakes. The glossy magazine covers and stories on television we aspire to be like are apparently about perfect people. We glorify those images and put those people on a pedestal, as an ideal, almost at a godly standard. We are often surprised and scandalized when they fall from those lofty places as if that never happens to anyone. Unfortunately, this is a vestige of the industrial revolution. A time where machines were expensive and inaccessible, and where a single error, such as a production line stoppage or mistakes in the manufacturing process, had a significant impact on the company's reputation and often ability to survive.

In today's world, people should be trained differently. Making mistakes is acceptable. While some mistakes can have terrible consequences, we must remember to prioritize the process over the results and tailor it based on the context. In fact, people tend to learn more effectively from

their failures, rather than replicating a successful recipe exactly as it was created. The power to innovate comes from having the freedom to ask questions and by implementing a process of trial and error. **The faster you can learn to fail, the better your learning becomes. Depending on the criticality of the job we are looking to master, we need to keep on failing and improving incrementally until we have developed a core competency.** Babies do not give up on walking the first time they fail to stand up; they keep trying until they get it right. So, why do we expect perfection from people?

I have had the privilege of learning a lot of things in my life and career: many successes and some massive failures. From my experiences, the only thing I can take away is to be a lifelong learner with no attachments to success or failure. I have learned to let go, surrender, and not take any success or failure for granted. Life is a learning process, and with it comes being able to manifest amazing things from time to time.

The real problem was that these essential life skills were never taught to me during school, college, or in my early career. The focus was always on doing certain things right, at a level where the employers got their work done with less effort and investment. While this sounds like a good plan on the surface, it subsequently leads to massive failures. When employees decide to venture out on their own or attain leadership positions, they find themselves striking out as they haven't really had any exposure to the skills necessary to lead and succeed. Since they are expected to be the ones that others are looking up to, it becomes a case of the blind leading the blind. It also leads to organizational politics, like others who may be good at some area that you are weak in now taking shots at getting your job. If this sounds familiar, read on.

I believe the real problem is that people stop learning, forget how to learn, or don't know what they need to learn. The other challenge is a certain arrogance associated with people, young and old, as they seem to have the "I know it all" attitude. The reality is that it is an inferiority complex masquerading as a superiority complex, to hide the fact that they really do not know. It is an "impostor syndrome" where the fear is that others will find out the true extent of their knowledge or lack thereof. In a world that values knowledge and correlates social superiority with it, it can be threatening to someone who is not secure in themselves. On the other hand, imagine if the leaders were uncompromising in their core values but were willing to admit their failures, where they were wrong, and what they don't know. Vulnerability is such a refreshing change in this era of false pride, arrogance, and shiny toys that are purely for showing off.

The reality is that almost anyone can learn to do practically anything if they commit themselves to master that area. Surrounding yourself with the right mentors and guides, as well as supportive friends and family who will cheer you on to success, are essential to reach any desired outcome. Choose wisely. Spend some time developing your moral compass, define what your core values are, what you stand for, and what you are willing to fight for, and associate with the people who align with those core values.

During my school days, I did well and was successful, not because I was the best, but mostly because others did not really aim high enough. It was very apparent when I moved to a new high school and then college that the community that I had now entered consisted of students who knew that game a lot better than I did. It was even more apparent when I went into engineering and higher studies that my weaknesses would get amplified in the community of those who were certainly more disciplined. Through sheer hard work and persistence and having a mindset that associated no shame with failures, I have been able to shrug those off and keep going.

Sometimes, life might knock you out. If you can wobble back on your feet before the count hits ten, you are able to fight another round. You may get bruised along the way, the ego more than the body. As a good friend of mine and mentor, Forbes Riley, would say, "*Think of your ego as a foreman who is trying to protect you from what it believes will hurt you. It does not know any better other than the patterns that it has seen so far. If you are willing to stretch out of your comfort zones, then what happens is that your capacity to absorb these shocks and recover becomes even larger.*"

In my case, it was some mega successes, more attributed to being in the right place at the right time. Not having the wisdom to understand that, what followed were years of trying to replicate luck. It took the form of investing into a business path that was rocky, where what you gained in the first step soon disappeared and then some. You swing from a positive territory where you could have retired at your young age to someone who must worry about paying off massive debts during their mid-life. Forget about typical measures of societal success. It's certainly not something parents advocate for their children, but I am lucky that my parents, spouse, her parents, and son have always been supportive, even when it got tough.

One thing that was always constant despite the ups and downs was my faith in God. While I was not highly active in church, one verse that my grandfather taught me as a child was Psalm 23: "*The Lord is my Shepherd; I shall not want.*" If the birds and the animals have food and shelter, why should we as humans worry? In fact, FEAR is an acronym for "False Emotion Appearing Real." Fear is also a tool used to keep people under the control of the enemy. Fear is a temporary tool, and, **when people reach a breaking point, they have often been able to fight their oppressors and break free.**

Fear is like a baby elephant tied down with a metal chain. The elephant refuses to break free from the thin rope it is tied down with, even when it becomes a huge beast. It remembers the past experiences and believes that resistance is futile and gets comfortable with being domesticated, the idea of humans feeding them on a regular basis, and not having to do things on their own.

Along the same lines, if we can get our students to fail earlier during school, such as with experiential projects, the deeper and stronger their learning becomes while the stakes aren't as high. In our massively successful training program for bringing minority women and veterans who never had an opportunity to do computer science or other advanced college degrees into the IT field, we are able to not only teach them skills that help them get a job as a software programmer, but we are also able to coach them on the growth mindset necessary to be successful in their lives and careers. We have been able to apply this model of outcome-based learning across several countries, cultures, and language boundaries, helping thousands of young men, women, and even mid-career veterans find new opportunities with some of the most advanced IT organizations in the world.

What we have discovered is that anyone can learn anything, provided they have a growth mindset and are open to learning. If someone is willing to work hard to achieve the skills needed to be successful and surround themselves with the right mentors, every failure will lead to a larger success. The other key learning that we can take away is that **"learning to learn" is a master skill**, just as important as "learning to communicate." Unfortunately, this is not taught in our school system.

Many schools teach students to pass an examination, which is supposed to measure their success in learning. In fact, many training programs confuse teaching with learning. Transfer of learning involves the acquisition of knowledge and being able to apply that in practice on their own or in collaboration with others. Learning should not be about regurgitating information by a midnight deadline but should be taking the information and allowing students to experiment and put their ideas into practical use. This requires an environment that is accepting of failures and allows students to make as many mistakes as possible when in school. **Isn't an expectation of perfection and a fear of failure what causes so many people to reach their fullest potential? The more failures you have in a safe environment, the higher the successes in other places.**

If the consequences for failure are not catastrophic, the mentors, teachers, and managers can be there to guide them toward higher and better outcomes. We, as students, should not be motivated by a grade but rather by how much we are able to absorb and apply the learning. **In the process, we unleash the creativity of the people and come up with world-changing ideas because we are open to inputs from others and are not afraid to try things. It is not about whose idea it was; rather, it**

is about how we collaborate and create a better outcome for all the participants, including themselves, their organizations, their customers, and the rest of the world.

If you are in any kind of leadership position, whether it is school, a professional setting, or within your family, remember that learning and thriving requires a learning culture where everyone values the fact that no one knows everything and dedicates time to learning and experimenting. **Do not be afraid to fail.**

This will lead to happier lives, as you are not trying to be better than your neighbor; you are able to learn with them. Rather, be committed to continuous improvement and growth so that the future versions of yourself can be the best versions possible. This idea helps to diminish pressure away from people and how they have been programmed. **Live your life with integrity and strive to be better today than yesterday. Past is past, and tomorrow is not a given, so make today better than yesterday. Day by day, it will add up, and the compounding effect is phenomenal.**

Instead of telling people you can't, or you aren't able to, try to provide learning tools and create opportunities for people to take baby steps. When they fall, encourage them to get back up and try again. Soon, they will be crawling, walking, running, and before you know it, they will be driving, and some may even fly you all the way to the moon or Mars and beyond. As Steve Jobs wrote, "The journey is **the reward.**" Indeed.

Sunil Cherian

Sunil Cherian is a Silicon Valley CEO, investor, mentor, and advisor to startups and can be frequently found coaching business owners and families on financial literacy and supporting his wife on her journey to business ownership as a financial consultant and service provider and being the biggest cheerleader for his son to find and follow his passion.

He is also passionate about learning and serves as an advisor to some nonprofits who support the colleges and universities that he has been affiliated with. He is hopeful of transferring some of the learning mindset to the next generation of leaders and their teachers who influence them. He has a bachelor's in technology from College of Engineering, Trivandrum, India, and a master's in computer science from SUNY-Albany, and has spent nearly thirty years in the technology and related fields. You can connect with him on LinkedIn at **https://linkedin.com/in/sunil-cherian** or Facebook at **https://www.facebook.com/sunil.cherian.77**.

He is a co-founder and CEO of Copperwire Systems (**https://copperwire.io**). Copperwire Systems is your bridge between the blockchain and all the efficiency, security, and visibility benefit it can provide to logistics, procurement, finance, and more. It provides the technology, application, and middleware services to make blockchain accessible and increase enterprise "blockchain conductivity."

He is also the founder and CEO of Mentor Global (**https://mentor-global.com**), a company that pioneered and evolved the idea of outcome-based learning. With its customer and partner, UST Global, they successfully launched the "STEP IT UP America" initiative, which has led to over one thousand minority women and veterans get IT jobs with Fortune-500 companies.

Prior to this, he was a founding team member of Array Networks and was a key member of the management team that took the company public. He started his technology career in the US with VMX and was eventually part of Octel Communications and Lucent Bell Labs.

Part 3: Step into Your Power

LIVING A LIFE WITH GINSIINMEI - TRUTH, GOODNESS AND BEAUTY - IN TIMES OF CHAOS AND DISTRESS

BY MARSHA CHEUNG GOLANGCO

Since the global pandemic started in late 2019, the world has been placed in an unprecedented domain of fear and anxiety: The very fabric of all societies was immensely impacted. With lockdowns and the fear of getting sick, daily reports of deaths and high unemployment, and the social unrest that follows, the emotions are in constant distress.

When will these nightmares end? When will we return to normal? Many of us are already missing the "good old days" when the big news was about the ups and downs of the stock market, the lifestyles of the rich and famous, and having fun. But these days, the sad, unspoken truth for many is that the era of feeling completely safe and secure is over—at least, for the time being. The normal, good old days are not returning soon.

Until the peaceful times return, we are living in a state of chaos and distress with continuous, nagging feelings of fear and uncertainty. People react differently during times of crisis—some just want to hide at home, some want to fight and vent their anger, some lose their appetites, some stuff themselves with comfort foods, some have difficulty concentrating, and others suffer insomnia. There is a sense of losing the balance and control of a normal life. Given this situation and **the fact that we cannot change the world around us, perhaps we should look into ways we can alter our own state of mind and being**.

What can we do to make ourselves stronger and more stable, even in times of trouble like these?

The Power of Feng Shui

The ancient teaching of Feng Shui offers some infinite wisdom. **Feng Shui is a way of living in harmony with *our* surroundings**. It is believed that scattered energies cause instability and chaos, affecting *our* emotional stability and clarity: **Anxiety and fear occur when a person is in a low energy field or an unstable state. The origin of anxiety can be both internal and external.** When Chi—the universal life force—is raised, a human body is in a higher energy state, and a person is physically, mentally, and emotionally empowered. This person now becomes stronger, more stable, more courageous, and thus more capable of confronting challenges and adversities with increased energy. One of the basic purposes of Feng Shui is to increase the vibrancy of a physical space to bring in the beneficial Chi and deflect the negative Chi, leading to a person's physical vitality and mental clarity.

There are simple steps we can follow to alter our physical environment, leading to a transformation of our mental and emotional state. The essence of these basic techniques is to create an environment that facilitates the circulation and accumulation of beneficial, positive Chi and to neutralize harmful, negative Chi. The desired environment is both harmonious and balanced.

The three basic techniques are:

1. **Clarification**: a clean space helps in clearing the mind and calming the heart

2. **Simplification**: an uncluttered space helps in simplifying life

3. **Organization**: create order out of chaos in your environment

Clarification is a process of cleaning up the living environment, both exterior and interior. Inside the house, any objects that are dirty, dusty, or smelly should be cleaned or removed. Carpets should be vacuumed; lighting fixtures, windows, and floors should be cleaned frequently. In the yard, any dead leaves, tree branches, and shrubs should be cleared to make way for a new life. A periodic fresh layer of paint can be applied on the inside and outside walls, giving the building a fresh new look. **A clean environment helps to keep the space fresh and vibrant, increasing the Chi level to empower the people who live in it.** It is also important to keep the center of the house clean and vibrant by avoiding the placement of bathrooms or storage rooms in this area. Improper placement of "negative" structures and objects in this critical location affects the general well being of the inhabitants. Also, when a person is in distress, a simple breathing exercise or meditation will help to calm the heart and clear the mind.

Simplification is a process of reducing the number of objects in a given space. **When space is overly cluttered, it decreases the speed of Chi circulation.** As a result, the life force is diminished, rendering the space stagnant. In general, it is difficult for human beings to give up possessions that have monetary or sentimental value. The ability to let go of some physical objects helps to let go of the complexity in one's own life. Many people have very busy schedules and extremely hectic lives. **This process**

will help them to simplify their lives, reducing their stress and anxiety. It is important to note that having too many paper goods in a space depletes the lifeforce in that area. Therefore, old newspapers and magazines should be recycled or discarded periodically.

Organization is a process of creating order and harmony in a space. **When a space is full of objects that are scattered all over, it generates scattered energies that affect the physical stability and balance of a person. As a result, a person is less focused mentally and more agitated emotionally**. To better manage one's life, setting priorities and scheduling one's time are effective tools in organization. In Feng Shui, the act of organizing a given space, whether it is a garage, a desk, or a closet, harmonizes that space and helps to organize a person's thoughts or emotions. These are a few examples of Feng Shui techniques in creating a powerful living environment during times of crisis or chaos. Feng Shui is an effective system in harmonizing a space, making it more stable and organized. **As a result, people feel more at ease and energized, regardless of the world events that might be happening around them. Using Feng Shui, a person can always feel calm, centered, and at peace. When we are at the optimal state of our being, we will get in touch with the inner power of GinSiinMei that already exists within us.**

The Power of GinSiinMei
Truth Goodness Beauty

GinSiinMei is the highest level of quality of life known in ancient Chinese culture for thousands of years. It is a collective energy field of three important qualities: Gin, Siin, and Mei.

Gin by itself is truth: a state of quality of being true

Siin by itself is goodness: the quality of being good

Mei by itself is beauty: the quality of being beautiful

These three qualities do not separate themselves; rather, the synergy of all three will act together to bring out the best possible outcomes.

To empower the world with GinSiinMei starts with ourselves; we are the source of this power. When we are being GinSiinMei, we are in the domain of loving-kindness with compassion. We will act with GinSiinMei and do GinSiinMei deeds, resulting in a world of GinSiinMei. Having a world GinSiinMei is fulfilling our ultimate vision of living a way of life that is beneficial to all living matters in our world.

We all have GinSiinMei within us; it is a matter of connecting with this inner power. It starts with us being healthy physically, mentally, and spiritually. When we have a loving heart and a clear mind, we become aware of the inner power within us.

We are the source of our GinSiinMei

As mystical as it is, we do not know how GinSiinMei works. A conscious awareness would be a start, then a conscious choice of a desire for GinSiinMei will evolve. It is just like lighting the first candle in a dark room, causing the rippling effect to eventually light up the whole room. We are the source of this power, generating from within and sharing from self to ignite others to get in touch with theirs, eventually transforming the world.

Just imagine what the world would be if we all live a life constantly in touch with the power of GinSiinMei, serving humanity and contributing to the world that we all love and live in!

A Personal GinSiinMei Journey

My life is like living through the natural rhythm of the natural world, with ups and downs and changes of the four seasons. I learn from early childhood to appreciate the constant changes and the twists and turns of life.

As an immigrant originally from Hong Kong, I have been living in my adopted country of the United States for many decades. In the beginning, I had a range of diverse viewpoints in different aspects of life and many contrasting feelings. Despite the differences between the Eastern and Western cultures, I am always able to find a balance of peace and harmony. **I find life is like navigating a river with so many twists and turns, so many surprises and challenges, yet so many accomplishments and rewards. I have always been able to maintain a focus on "hoping for the best and preparing for the worst."** That is one of the many timeless bits of wisdom that I learned from my traditional Chinese family while growing up in Hong Kong during the British Colonial Era.

As a longtime business owner specializing in sustainable green designs and environmental Feng Shui consulting, I encountered many challenges while creating and building my business. It is not a traditional line of work. It is totally different from the conventional college degrees that I received with majors in biology, ecology, home economics, and environmental science. My life turned out to be completely different than what my family expected for me, and perhaps what I expected for myself. Today, due to my many years of experience, I am considered a Feng Shui expert in the new-home-building industry. I have also written three books, *The Power of Feng Shui Trilogy*. I am also a life coach and a motivational speaker, sharing valuable lessons from a life journey of challenges, struggles, and triumphs.

As a lifetime community leader, I am committed to a sustainable world of truth, goodness, and beauty for all people. Because of this commitment, I continue to develop a local to global collaboration through my sustainable green Feng Shui work as well as community advocacy. I continue

to live a proactive and productive life, not willing to stop growing and developing, despite the fear of getting old, sick, and dying. I have a deep intention of completing my cycle of life by fulfilling my true purpose: to be of service to humanity and make my contribution to the world! How can you bring more GinSiinMei (TruthGoodnessBeauty) in your life?

To learn more about Feng Shui with *The Power of Feng Shui Trilogy* written by Marsha Cheung Golangco, here are the titles of the three books:

- *The Power of Feng Shui for Builders*: To honor all legendary builders in the world.
- *The Power of Feng Shui for Your Life*: To honor all empowered women in the world.
- *The Power of Feng Shui for Green Living*: To honor all pioneers of the green movement who brought forth the possibility of a vital and healthy planet.

Marsha Cheung Golangco

Author, speaker, and social entrepreneur, Marsha is a longtime community advocate. Her mission is to promote a harmonious world that works for all. Since 1988, Marsha has used her knowledge and wisdom in helping her clients to create favorable and healthy living environments for a better quality of life. Her services include new home subdivision development, office buildings, businesses, workplace, and individual homes. Her clients came from all sectors of society—people who have a desire to better their lives.

Committed to a lifetime contribution to the ongoing sustainable green movement, Marsha continues to develop a local to global collaboration through her business and community advocacy. As a former human relations commissioner, she sees herself as a bridge, connecting her Asian American heritage to all communities.

Marsha actively participates in a diversity of community groups, including a board chair of APAPA Tri-Valley Chapter and a cofounder of Sustainable Contra Costa County. Marsha received numerous awards, including the President's Award of the Year of the Building Industry Association for her dedication to the advancement of professional women in the building industry and also an Honorable Mention Martin Luther King, Jr., Humanitarian Award of the Year for her numerous community contributions.

Marsha is the author of *The Power of Feng Shui Trilogy*:

- *The Power of Feng Shui for Builders*
- *The Power of Feng Shui for Your Life*
- *The Power of Feng Shui for Green Living*

Emails: **fengshu888@aol.com** or **mgolangco@gmail.com**
Websites: **www.windwater888.com** and **www.GolangcoGlobal.com**
Facebook: **https://www.facebook.com/GreenFengShuiConsulting**
LinkedIn: **https://www.linkedin.com/in/marsha-golangco-a192a11/**

EMPOWERED SOULS
BY YVONNE MUGHAL

With fast steps, I walked into my bedroom closet, seeking privacy in the farthest corner of the house. My heart was filled with heavy emotions weighing on my body as I dropped to my knees on the floor and allowed the tears and sobs to break forth. I started to cry uncontrollably. The emotions in my body needed to be released. Yet, I didn't understand. I just surrendered to the urge in my body that had gripped me just a few minutes earlier. As I bent over my knees, wailing sounds flowed out of me while tears streamed down my cheeks. The vocal and physical release eased the tension inside of me and the heaviness in my heart. After a minute that seemed like an eternity, the heaving motion subsided. I started to feel lighter in my chest, and my breathing calmed. But a big question remained: Why was I crying? What did it mean? What had just happened to me? I had no answers.

I walked into the bathroom to wash my face and looked into the mirror, staring at my own questioning eyes. As I walked back upstairs into the kitchen, the telephone rang. "Hello?" I answered with my usual calm voice.

There was hysterical crying on the other side as I listened to our oldest daughter.

"Little Gabi died. She is dead. I did CPR on her. I called the ambulance. I did everything I could. She is dead. Mutti, I don't know what to do."

I listened to her frantic voice as peace flowed through my body. My heart filled with the desire to hug her, hold her in my arms, and calm her down. At the same time, something deep inside of me resonated with the shocking news and the panic in her voice and ignited a rush of adrenaline that caused my heart to pound. Suddenly, my breathing turned shallow as my whole body vibrated to Aliya's feelings.

"Where are you, Aliya? Let me come over. Papa will be home in a few minutes, and we will both come," I replied with a steady voice to help calm her down.

Aliya, my oldest stepdaughter, was earning her living as a nanny. She was tending six children between the ages of a few months to two years old at her younger sister's home. Zara had gone back to working full-time in a successful and well-paying career as an accountant after the birth of her first child. The sisters had worked out an arrangement that supported them both. Aliya was tending her nephew, her own two-year-old son, and four other children in Zara's home.

Before I could call my husband, the phone rang again. Answering, I recognized Zara's voice. Calmer than her sister, she started to fill me in with more details. "Mutti. The medics are at our house. Aliya had found little Gabi facedown on the floor when she went to check on her. She had put her in the children's room for a nap, and she must have fallen out of her rocker. When she picked her up, she wasn't breathing. We prayed so hard that she would be okay, but she is dead. She is my co-worker's child. I feel so bad." I felt the sadness and fear of both of my stepdaughters and grieved for Gabi's parents' loss of their child.

Half an hour later, my husband and I sat in Zara's home, listening to the descriptions of the events of that day and the concerns of Zara and her husband regarding possible lawsuits from the grieving parents, which thankfully never happened.

Finally, upon returning home that evening and sharing the events with our three teenagers at home, I had time for myself to contemplate my feelings and physical body responses during the afternoon. As I thought back to my emotional breakdown in my closet, I wondered about its meaning. ***Had I felt Aliya's stressful feelings in the very moment she experienced them? Was there a deep emotional connection between us that I had not been fully aware of?*** Out of my three stepchildren, I had felt the least acceptance from her, and we seemed to have the weakest emotional bond with each other. From the time my husband's three children from his first marriage moved into our home to become a permanent part of our family, I felt a sense of competition and rejection from her, as if she was clearly letting me know, "You are not my mother." So, it surprised me that I had felt her so strongly.

It had all begun five years earlier. At age forty-four, I was entering the phase of perimenopause. I became more concerned about my health and sought the help of a holistic physician. It was during my visits with her that I discovered how numb I had become to my own feelings, needs, and desires. During a unique consultation intended to help me to discover the blocks to my feelings, I recalled a childhood memory. At age seven, my family moved to a new apartment, and for the first time, I had my own room. The moment I remembered was a sunny day, and I was joyfully playing with my eight-year-old brother as my mother opened the door filled with rage toward him. Our idyllic play was abruptly ended as I watched in shock at her uncommon yelling, beating, and kicking of my brother. I had never thought of it since except for a laughing conversation with my two brothers as young adults over our mother's loss of temper. What I had not realized until now is how that one-time event had caused a soul fracture within myself. **As I voiced the memory of this moment in the accepting and non-judging presence of my doctor, I felt a part of my soul returning into my heart.** As

I left her clinic that day, I felt a new and unfamiliar feeling: wholeness, an unusual sense of joy and freedom. I felt like I was walking on air.

During the following weeks, I felt a dull ache in my chest, and as I accepted the feeling in my body with gratitude, my heart seemed to expand as the doors of heaven appeared to open, and I felt surrounded by divine love. None of my family around me seemed to notice, and I had no words to describe what I was feeling and experiencing. **New awareness and understanding filled my mind. Any feelings of contention melted away between myself and my family members.** I cherished and basked in this new feeling and the warmth of heaven's love, and within its presence, I connected deeply with my own soul and felt an intense love for God, for people, and for the earth as a gift from our shared creator.

When January came, the warm and comforting presence of heaven withdrew, and I found myself surrounded by the reality of everyday life. I fell into a deep and dark depression or what is often referred to as the dark night of the soul. I wanted to die. I wanted my life to end. And that shocked me too. Where were all of these emotions coming from?

It took all of my willpower and telling myself over and over again: "I choose to live. I choose to live" to bring energy into my body and command it to move so I could return to my usual routine of supporting my husband and our children through my roles as a mother and housewife.

For the next year, I struggled emotionally and physically and tried through dietary changes and nutritional supplements to bring my body into wellness and myself returning to the joy, love, and peace I had so vividly and tangibly experienced. **Doing things for myself that I enjoyed started to fill my "empty cup." I had been so used to being there for my husband and our children, but not for myself. As I returned to activities that fed my spirit and were important to me, I returned to an inner sense of peace.**

The following summer, Aliya surprised me with an unexpected phone call: "Mutti, I am pregnant. I want to come over on Father's Day and tell Daddy." I heard the excitement in her voice. For a moment, my heart seemed to stop as a warning thought popped into my mind: *Not a good idea. Your father is still recovering emotionally from your announcement of getting divorced.* With my husband's background growing up in an Islamic family in Pakistan and I growing up in a Christian family in Germany, we both had strong standards and beliefs about family life.

"Aliya," I answered with a firm voice, "do not come over and tell Daddy that you are pregnant." There was a pause on the phone, followed by a disappointing question and an angry tone in her voice: "Why? Why can't I come?" I felt the frustration and anger emanating from her and remained calm and firm as I answered: "Daddy is not ready for this. Please do not come. Let me tell him that you are pregnant."

During an afternoon walk in East Canyon, I opened the topic to my husband. He already knew from the other children and immediately replied with his disappointment and grief over her behavior and that he did not want to see her. As I listened, my heart felt heavy, and I let out a soft sigh. I understood. My husband's voice had been clear, direct, and firm. "It hurts me to see her and what she does with her life. I can't bear it." It was his way to deal with the heartache. In the following months, we had very little contact with our oldest daughter.

In December, Aliya called me: "Mutti, I want you to come to the birth of my son." Her joyfulness was still apparent. I paused for a moment as the answer came from deep inside of my heart. "Yes, I will come. Call me when you are in the hospital."

A few days later, I opened the door to her delivery room. I was momentarily surprised by the presence of a young man whom Aliya introduced to me as her boyfriend. He appeared tense yet supportive. I greeted him briefly as I sat next to him on the couch. It felt strange, but I put my feelings aside to focus on Aliya and the birth of our first grandchild. Her joy over becoming a mother was present, and I wanted to celebrate with her. Within the next half-hour, our first grandson was born. I was so grateful to be there.

Three years later, I enrolled in a year long course learning about emotional release work. Since my experience with heaven, I often felt overcome by anxiety and an accompanying shaking in my body. I longed to be with people yet strangely could also feel suddenly overwhelmed by no apparent reason at all. **The fluctuating emotional experiences and accompanying sensations in my body were a mystery to me.**

It was late January 2013 as I participated in a weekend training of learning and assisting other women and men ranging from their early twenties to eighty years old with the unique emotional healing modality taught in the course. On that Saturday afternoon, as I focused on my two-year-old inner child, I became aware of feelings and thoughts that had formed even at such a young age. At the time, my mother had given birth to a full-term stillborn son and returned home without the joy of a newborn child in our home. **As the facilitator guided me through the emotional experiences of my two-year-old self, I discovered layers of unprocessed grief that my soul and body were connected to.** After identifying and removing each layer of feelings that were present in my home at the time, I realized a core belief I had formed at that time. My baby brother, whom I had often missed throughout my life, got to go back home to heaven while I had to remain on earth. Tears flowed from my eyes with this awareness. Another soul fracture had caused a disconnection from my body, zapping me of vital joy and life force energy within myself. **After the session, I felt filled with light, love, and joy. I knew the work had great potential for uplifting hearts and healing soul wounds, and bringing vitality and strength to the body.**

As I continued to assist others in their personal healing journey, I discovered how my body connected to the feelings of others. As I thought back on the moment in the closet and my uncontrollable crying, I realized that I had not only connected to the emotional pain of Aliya but also of myself, my mother, and my great grandmother who had lost four sons to war, illness, and intercontinental relocation.

As unusual as the moment was and as strange as it appeared and felt, it was nothing but a releasing of grief that was held in my body, in the very fibers of my cells. The freeing moment came when I recognized that I had connected not only to my stepdaughters emotional pain in the very moment of her experience but also to the pain of my ancestors during different times of their life. Their deep grief was still stored within my body. When I recognized that the emotional healing could begin. The renewing of my physical strength in my body and all of my tissues and cells could start. What seemed like a breakdown was actually a breakthrough and an opening to joy, love, peace, and unity within my body, soul, and spirit.

We each carry within ourselves a deep reservoir of inner wisdom, strength, and resilience. However, due to fear and a lifetime of conditioning and learning to fit into cultural and societal expectations, most of us never birth the untapped potential of our unique soul with its power and purpose. The time is now to tap into our deepest yearning and reclaim the love and light within ourselves and share it with the world.

The soul fracturing we experience throughout our life is real, but so is the truth of the healing power of reclaiming who we are and why we live now. I urge you to seek the empowering and integrative work of energy kinesiology and soul restoration modalities.

Yvonne Mughal

Yvonne was born in communist East Germany to a Christian family. She experienced religious discrimination and oppression of freedom and creativity while learning to be true to her faith and maneuver the complexities of human dictatorships. She immigrated to the United States in 1985 after enduring a period of political threats and persecutions.

In 1989, Yvonne married her husband, Tariq, who had been born into a Muslim family and grew up in Pakistan. Yvonne welcomed Tariq's three children into their home and family with an open heart. The challenge of being a stepmother while also learning to be a mother to three children with her husband taught her many lessons.

She spent most of her adulthood taking care of home and family while learning to adapt to American life as an immigrant, the wife of a Pakistani-American professor, and bringing multiple cultures together in peace and harmony. Her greatest joy has been to be a mother of all of her children.

In 2008, with the assistance of a holistic physician, she connected to a part of her soul and experienced four weeks of remarkable connection with divine love, light, and presence. The experience taught her that each of us exists for a greater purpose beyond ourselves and that our greatest joy and fulfillment comes from discovering and living our personal service to humanity.

Since 2013, Yvonne has learned about her gift of empathy and how to assist others in reclaiming their spiritual identity and the gifts they were born with so they can step into their personal magnificence, purpose, and contribution to the world.

She and her husband enjoy traveling, camping, and the outdoors. They currently have seven grandchildren.

Facebook: Mind Body Heart Connection
Email: **mbh2integrate@gmail.com**
Phone: +1 801-949-5859

I PLAYED A DIFFERENT HAND
BY SHERENA SMITH

During my journey as a child born in Little Rock, Arkansas, I was often told that I wouldn't succeed nor make it through high school without getting pregnant. These words pushed me to want to strive to prove this statement to be wrong. I was determined to ensure I made the difference by completing high school and to not have children until I got married.

I was a product of a single parent who didn't always get it right but did what she felt was right at the time. I was the oldest of three and the only girl of my mother. My dad was my hero and the first man I looked up to as to what a man should be like. I was always excited to see my dad and to talk to him. I lived with my grandparents until around the age of seven, when my mother married my stepdad. **My upbringing involved domestic abuse amongst my mother, my siblings, and me. I was blessed to leave that environment to get to live with my grandparents while in the seventh thru ninth grades.** I participated in many organizations in junior high school, such as basketball, president of the Future Business Leaders of America, drill team, and many more. **My grandparents were my support system encouraging me daily.** My heart ached daily, knowing that my brother was still in a toxic environment, and I was with my grandparents obtaining a work permit to work at McDonald's and a learner's permit at the age of fourteen, driving to work weekly. I was living the time of my life with support from my grandparents, attending my games, shows, and performances.

During the second semester of my ninth-grade year, my mother graduated from college and moved to Dallas, separate from my stepdad. I was then afforded the opportunity to move back with my mother and siblings to Dallas, Texas. This was a highlight in my life as I missed them. After a few months, my stepdad moved to Dallas and moved in. Things were still bad, but I stayed through the graduation of high school.

Immediately following graduation, I enrolled in college and was able to graduate undergrad without any kids. I married in 1997 and had a kid a year after marriage. On August 4, 1996, my son was born to my husband and me. **My marriage ended up being a repeat of my past life involving domestic violence. My son witnessed the very things I wanted to shield him from as a kid. I knew that the environment was not a healthy one to bring up a son and something had to be done.**

In 2004, my husband and I separated and eventually decided to divorce, which is never an easy decision, given we had a child so young and in elementary school at the time. Although it was a tough time for my son and me, we were able to cope as best we could and move forward with life as we knew it. This meant it was only my son and me embarking on this journey together.

Due to my son being a timid and quiet child, he made friends in our neighborhood that he attended school with. On many occasions, my house was the home to all the neighborhood kids, which would come spend many weekends. There were times that my son would go to their homes, but often, they were at our home. I would communicate regularly with the parents as

I looked after their kids and continued to ensure everyone was okay and safe. Often, you hear the words, "it takes a village," and I am a living witness to that. When my son was with his friends, he would brighten up.

One summer, my son attended a summer camp and was being bullied and decided he would react by pushing the kid, which was totally out of character for him. The coach at the program spoke to me about the incident and advised that after speaking with him, he had learned that my son was angry due to his dad fighting his mom. **He decided to take my son on as his mentee. I was so blessed to have the coach take out the time to mentor my son and talk with him regularly.**

The next obstacle was while applying to middle school, a test was required; my son tested and scored very high on the test. I was told that he would be contacted with the next steps for admission. I was later contacted and told that he wasn't selected to attend the school. When I inquired as to why he wasn't accepted, I was told that they ran out of spots; however, there were children that scored lower and applied after my son. I appealed the decision, and my son could enroll in the school.

On a positive note, while in middle school, my son was able to join the band, which really allowed him the opportunity to meet other students and work on music together. As the school year progressed, I could tell that he was coming around with being more outspoken and engaged. As the years passed, my son was becoming more and more independent.

At high school enrollment time, a test was required again in order to be accepted. He was accepted to attend the high school and joined the band. During his tenure in the band, he had the opportunity to serve as section leader of his instrument. Additionally, over the years, he learned to play many instruments and to dance while playing them. His band director was a great mentor to him.

After completing high school, he went on to attend college at Samford University to pursue a dual degree in physics engineering and electrical engineering through a program with UAB. While in his second year of college, my father—his grandfather—committed suicide. This was a shocking and hurtful time for us all. We have all missed him year over year and will never understand, but we know that we must move forward while keeping him in our hearts. He always spoke about attending my son's graduation and being so proud of him. We have had a tough journey but looked forward to graduation in 2020 (December).

I have chosen to tell my story in the event there is someone out there that needs encouragement and/or to hear a positive story; just because you are a single parent, it is not the end of the world. You can still become successful and live out your dreams if you keep the faith. You are not on this journey alone.

I have been mentoring single parents as my mission and offering mentorship and assistance in resume writing, donating suits, and providing free webinars to those wanting to enhance their knowledge in business and project management. Additionally, those that don't have a college degree can obtain certification through my services to enhance knowledge, pay, and confidence.

You don't have to be a product of your past or environment if it wasn't so pleasant. You are in control of your own destiny and future. Dream big and research what it would take to be what you desire to be. This would be the first step in embarking on starting your journey in fulfilling your dreams. Set goals and provide realistic dates for achieving each of your goals. As part of your research, search salaries for the desired titles. Ensure to research if the title typically requires a degree, and if you don't have a degree, research certifications in that field.

If you are part of a domestic violence relationship and it doesn't get better with apologies for every incident, if the person is only talking

and not seeking professional help, it will continue to happen repeatedly. Ladies, you are worth so much more than living in a toxic relationship. It is important to find peace and happiness. This sometimes includes meditating, unwinding in a hot tub, lighting candles, or vacations to your favorite places. If vacations are impossible, find a picture to imagine being at and relax. If you can treat yourself to a spa, it helps with relaxation. If a spa is not possible, create your own atmosphere for an in-home spa day.

There are many support groups to meet you exactly where you are. Don't ever feel that you are locked into a situation without options. You are worthy and important to our society. Continue to keep a positive mindset and strive to learn something new, if not daily, maybe weekly or monthly, to ensure you are continuing to grow. Remember that you are the kid's first role model. It is never too late to change direction if required.

Many see me today and think I just overnight became who I am today; however, I have endured many obstacles, heartbreaks, and challenges along my journey, but I'm still here learning daily and striving to be my best daily. **I encourage you to continue to strive for being the best that you can be and trusting that you can make changes for the better.**

Sherena Smith

Sherena is a versatile, accomplished, and dynamic Agile coach with over ten years of practical experience transforming organizations and managers at the portfolio- and program-levels. She is an expert in growing highly effective teams, guiding mission-critical work from concept to cash, and coaching Scrum masters, product owners, tech leads, and developers at the team level. She is a well-organized and proactive leader who is able to improve overall project management by increasing collaboration, innovation and introducing techniques that promote adaptability and flexibility in the face of unpredictable circumstances.

Sherena has successfully established and distributed Agile/Scrum, Scrum ban, and program level agile environment to support a $120M software development project. As a coach, she has developed and delivered team and organization training materials and workshops, building knowledge and skills to facilitate the Agile transformation. She established and supported communities of practices to promote organizational understanding of Agile roles and to help individuals develop into them. She has coached teams, Scrum masters, business analysts, managers, and executives on Agile values and principles to promote continuous improvement in practices and artifacts. She has championed cultural change and collaborated with other coaches on plans and techniques for accelerating and advancing the organization's transformation. She's mentored teams, leading them to be self-directed with strong accountability, decision making, conflict resolution, and transparency.

Sherena is certified in Lean, Agile, Product, and Project Portfolio Management by organizations such as PMI®, Scrum Alliance and SAFe Program Consultant, and Enablement on (Leading SAFe, SAFe for Teams, SAFe for Government, SAFe DevOps, SAFe POPM, SAFe-APM, SAFe-LPM, SAFe-SSM).

LinkedIn: **https://www.linkedin.com/in/sherenaysmith/**
Facebook: **https://www.facebook.com/sherena.smith.3/about**

STEPPING INTO MY POWER
BY UNA LAPPIN

It is a Friday afternoon in my place of work a couple of weeks before Christmas. I have just received an email from my manager to go to her office for a meeting about my contract. **I am six months pregnant with my second son, a wanted baby after two miscarriages.**

I take the lift today, as I am tired. I arrive, and as I go into her office, I walk past a member of HR. I think to myself; *this isn't good.*

To cut a very tearful and upsetting story short, my temporary contract is now not being extended, and I have until the end of March, approximately three months, to find a new job. I was reassured it was nothing to do with my standard of work but to do with efficiencies. I have been asking about my job for months previously and was constantly told there was no news—the last time I asked was eight weeks ago.

My heart is racing, my eyes are stinging with tears, my face is wet with tears, my hands are shaking, and I have a dry open mouth in shock. I am stuck to the chair, and the words that are being said to me are going over my head. If my life depended on them today, I could not remember them. I feel like the carpet has been pulled from under me while walking. I can't look at my manager. She keeps apologizing. I am told by the HR lady I should have been on the lookout for a job as my contract was not permanent—supportive! I try to speak, but no words come out. I need to go before I faint.

I leave the office a mess and a worry wart as I am pregnant for a start, and secondly, I am the main earner in my house, so my mind is not only thinking just of my baby, but also about the mortgage and everything else.

My manager comes down to my office a little while later, apologizing again and wishing she could have done something. Again, I am told it has nothing to do with my standard of work. Before I know it, I say, "Apologies won't pay my bills."

I am an extremely resilient, strong, and sometimes stubborn lady, but this broke me. I feel so let down and alone. I leave the office, holding back my tears as I pass the friendly security officer in reception. *Remain strong*, I am thinking, but what I want to do is shout from the rooftops that this is not fair or right.

That was in 2015. I take Christmas off and see in the New Year.

It is 2016. I am redeployed to a different role, new team, and new duties. I am not able to stay at my level I was at before, as there are no jobs available, so I agree, for want of trying to enjoy my pregnancy, to take what is available, sign the form for a new job, and go on maternity leave. In the signing, I am redeployed and demoted in a stroke of my pen.

I dropped almost half my salary and all managerial responsibilities. I am heartbroken. I love my job. I love the people I engage with across all of

Belfast, and they love me. They all are in shock, but not as much as me. **We as a family are also broke, but thankfully with family support and support from the bank, thanks to my attitude, we are shown compassion from a very understanding bank officer.**

Nine months later, I return to work, and rather than turn left into the building, I turn right. I am still breastfeeding my son to stay connected to him. It is hard as I need to continue to work full-time. For the first week, I cry each time I go into the bathroom. I am experiencing shame, embarrassment, anger, pain, guilt—name the emotion, I have it. I am in a bad place, and I am a pure worry wart. I continue this way, somehow, getting through each day believing this job will define me for the rest of my life. Before I know it, it is January 2019.

I am out with my family and one of my sisters. I finally find the strength to remove my mask and tell her everything. I drop my head, my guard, and cry hard, quietly, as I am in a public place. For the first time in years, when I am asked, "how are you," I decide to tell the truth. I have coped enough. We, as a family, have wasted enough of our time together worrying about everything. I am so upset, and I am right back to all the emotions I have not even acknowledged, never mind dealt with.

From that point on, I know I am going to be okay. I have finally opened up—the strong, independent, middle child that I am.

So here, my story picks up a lot, and at speed.

I am back at work after that conversation, and within a couple of months, I do what I should have done years ago—I phone in sick. I feel worthless, demoralized, and I am now hearing my story from someone else, and I am in disbelief.

I am angry with what happened. I am angry with myself for not doing this sooner. I am angry with everyone. I am tired, as I have been just surviving up to now. It may seem dramatic, but I was—I am not mentally challenged in work, and I am not socializing much as I am not a fun person to be around. Pride and "holding it all together and telling no one" did me no favors whatsoever.

I decide to finally act like a grown-up, stand in my power, and tell my parents the whole truth. I tell my brother, too. I am a private person, and I get on, but this needed other shoulders to lean on and ears to listen.

I ended up taking a full six months off, and you know, I am so proud of myself for doing that. I have family, medical, and union support, which I am grateful for, and as a result, I am paid in full. Knowing I have that support is a huge bonus, as it gives me time to rest, process my feelings, which were described by one of my counselors like a death, and discover my true calling in life—an international humanitarian.

During my six months off, I learn so much about myself. I feel better. I am sleeping again. I get my confidence and self-belief back. I truly believe my day job wouldn't define the rest of my life. The fog in my mind clears, many tears flow, and the awareness I've so much more to offer the world occurs. I process all my emotions, own what occurred, and close it off.

I have time to let the seed of realization sprout, and I discover deep down what I'm supposed to be doing with all my lived experiences as a humanitarian nutritionist from across two continents, Asia and Africa. I worked and lived in Afghanistan, Ethiopia, Angola, Kuwait, Iraq, Jordan, South Sudan, Niger, and the Democratic Republic of Congo.

And hence my transformation begins. I make lists and reach out and talk to so many supportive, kind, and understanding people. I rekindle old connections and then make lots of new ones, too. I stop counting to be honest, but each person sees the true Una, not the Una in her office. I am not able to be me in the office before I went off. My wings were clipped, and my voice muted. **I promise myself on my return that I will be the true**

Una—the positive, happy, upbeat, supportive, and energetic Una, the one I lost for a while as I was surviving.

The new friends and connections see my vision, my hope, my dream, and believe me. People offer me independent opportunities when they hear of my background. I realize that all my previous experiences have not gone away. I had not lost them. It is a joyful time.

I return to my day job six months later, a new lady, refreshed for a start, lighter and happier, and am known to whistle around the office. My wings are not clipped anymore, and my voice is not muted. My attitude and outlook are beyond my day job.

I am back a full year now, and so much has changed, and I am a completely new lady. I have coped, and due to that event, I am much stronger. I treat it now as a gift. If I had not been redeployed, I would never have had the time to think of my true calling and visit my attic one day and get lost in all my international wares. I do wish, though, I had started the "dealing with" process sooner, but I can't go back, only forward.

Today, as you read this chapter of mine, I have acted out my dream. I am the proud founder and director of my own business, Unique New Adventure, Ltd., which I established in April 2020 to "rejoice in our differences through education" thirteen years after my last humanitarian field experience. I am happy and, once again, full of passion and energy. I felt it was imperative to pass on my privileged education and learning of all things new, as I place a lot on the importance of humanity. I know the benefits personally in seeing people as people and being compassionate toward my fellow man and womankind. I see people as people. We are all different, but the same. We all look different, but beyond our skin and cultures, customs, religions, languages, food, and clothes, we are all human beings wanting to be loved. We all love the same, and we all hurt the same.

I have delivered multiple educational workshops, expert talks, global podcasts, videos, interviews, and storytelling from my lived experiences. I am looking forward to furthering this continual sharing of my privileged education from across the world with children and adults, with more adventures to come, including writing my memoirs from daily journals I kept to publishing. **I believe it is never too early or too late to think of others and learn and experience something new.**

I have the utmost confidence in myself now that I will succeed in all I create, including being a successful author of multiple books, making a difference, and giving back.

My Wise Words of Wisdom

This was a hard road for my family and me at the time. It was a strain on my mental, physical, emotional, and financial health, as well as my marriage, so being the educator that I am, I have some wisdom to pass on. My wisdom is clear and concise, as when I was in that place, I didn't need or want detail. My top five pieces of advice are:

1. **Sometimes, when challenges come your way, they are nothing to do with you.** This is hard to hear but true. You have no control over some decisions, and when you start to think that way, it is easier to accept change.

2. **Things do work themselves out.** They do, and we learn from the experiences and become stronger.

3. **Tell someone, sooner rather than later, if you aren't in a good place.** I waited too long, so don't do the same!

4. **Take each day at a time.** Take it day by day, as it is a marathon, not a sprint. Little steps until you are ready for bigger steps; your time will come.

5. **Talk to people who are like-minded and supportive.** You need people who will support you, not drag you down, so chose your friends wisely!

My Enlightening Encouragement

Life is interesting, and things do happen. At the beginning of my story, I believed my world was falling apart, and the new job was forever. I am still in this role, and my business and books are my side hustle, but my mind and outlook are different. That is my anecdote of encouragement, along with:

1. **It is okay to take time off.** It does not make you a weak person; it makes you a stronger, more focused person. Yes, I had support for the full six months, but after a couple of days off, I did start to feel better. If an environment is not good, you can control where you will be!

2. **Seek medical advice as soon as you can.** This is key for support for your place of work, and it is also validation that what you are feeling is what you should be feeling!

3. **Be honest with your feelings.** Honesty with everyone, but more so with yourself. You know you better than anyone else.

4. **Make a list of your achievements to remind yourself of who you are.** You can still do it. You still have that experience; you just aren't in that place right now.

5. **Be kind to yourself!** Easier said than done, but do it, as it is so important.

My Call to Action

My transformation, which is continuing, showed me that when times are tough, I become more grateful for my life and all that is in it. I also took time out for myself and discovered new things. I would like to share two actions. One you have heard before, gratitude, and the other is creativity.

1. **Gratitude: appreciate all you have**

Action: Take five minutes when you just wake up or before you go to sleep and write down three things you are grateful for daily. The idea is to stop and appreciate what you have rather than thinking about what you don't have, a shift in your perspective.

2. **Creativity**

Action: Discover a new hobby or pick up a hobby you have neglected. You must enjoy it; otherwise, you will not keep at it. It is certainly a way to let your mind wander away from what you are going through. Recently, I have started to write poems. I would like to share one I feel we all can show to ourselves and each other.

Compassion

C is for the CARE we pass on to others,
O is for the OBSERVATIONS we learn from our brothers,
M is for the MINDS we want to broaden,
P is for the PASSION we now need to draw on,
A is for the ADVANCEMENT we all want to make,
S is for the SERVICES we need to take,
S, again, is for the SORRYS we have committed,
I is for the INVITATIONS we have omitted,
O is for the OPPORTUNITIES, for us all to learn,
And **N** is for the NETWORKS, we all yearn.

Una Lappin

I am an international humanitarian. I am married with two boys, and I currently live in Belfast, Ireland. I have worked as a nutritionist across two continents, Asia and Africa, within a variety of countries, including Afghanistan, South Sudan, and Iraq, where I was responsible for implementing nutrition surveys, the delivery of feeding programs, and health promotion with GOAL Global, CONCERN Worldwide, ACTED, and UN World Food Program.

I am the founder/director of my own business, Unique New Adventure, Ltd., which I established in April 2020 to "rejoice in our differences through education." I have delivered educational workshops, expert talks, global podcasts, interviews, and storytelling from my lived humanitarian experiences. I am looking forward to furthering this continual sharing of my privileged education from across the world with children and adults, so I am also writing my memoirs from daily journals I kept when I worked internationally.

I was a community nutritionist researcher within the University of Newcastle upon Tyne, England, and locally, I have tackled health inequalities with Irish travelers and many communities with a focus on mental well-being, food/fuel poverty, homelessness, and health literacy.

I am a director of JoinHer Network, a voluntary member of the Royal College of GP NI Patient Group, and a CONCERN Worldwide ambassador.

I hold a diploma in industrial studies, a BTEC in Community Capacity Building Trainers Programme, a BSc Hons in food technology management from the University of Ulster, a master's degree of science in international nutrition at the University of Aberdeen, and I am the first author in a scientific publication; Tohill, U.R., Curtis, P.J., Adamson, A.J., Mathers,

J.C. (2001) Individual's perception of diet with regard to health compared with recorded intake. Proceedings of the Nutrition Society. 60, 181A. I am a published co-author in *The Business of Connection's* ENE *Anthology*, KMD Books, 2020.

Email: **unarlappin@gmail.com**
Facebook: **https://www.facebook.com/groups/592699688009136**
https://www.facebook.com/AdventureNew/
LinkedIn: **https://www.linkedin.com/in/unalappin/**
Twitter: @LappinUna
Instagram: **https://www.instagram.com/ulappin/**
YouTube: **https://www.youtube.com/channel/UC52IHhqldHHHpDQz-Irlkug**

LEARN, UNLEARN AND RELEARN: THE EVOLUTION MANTRA

BY UPENDRA GIRI

"Man is made by his belief. As he believes, so he is."
—The Bhagavad Gita

With a humble beginning in a small village, Rangpur, District Bulandshahr in Uttar Pradesh in Northern India, I now live in Silicon Valley with my family, but even today, when I visit my birth country, I can actually "smell" the country. India has a distinct fragrance—whether it be of camphor, incense, cows, people, food, cars, and anything you imagine. You are immersed in the country from the very first step you take outside the airplane. Every time I enter India, I feel a warm, gentle embrace, an embrace that carries me through until the end of the journey when I don't want to let go of the familiar warmth. As I leave the country, I leave with a heavy heart, yearning to return as quickly as possible, to immerse myself again in a place of pure magic. My village was free from the hustle and bustle of city life—peaceful, calm, quiet, and full of greenery where one could breathe fresh air. Everyone was so happy, playful, cooperative, and the highest degree of peace, love, and unity, hard to find in today's urban lifestyle. You could find love, compassion, and respect for each other while villagers happily lived in the small huts or a home made of clay or mud. The villagers were socially knit together; every evening, they assembled in the village "Chopal" with their "hukkas," and chatting and talking goes on till late the night. I spent my childhood years listening to **epic tales of Ramayana and Mahabharata**. **Focus on the process, not the outcome**; self-confidence is a fundamental quality to living an effective, empowered, and fulfilling life. I learned this at an early age from Bhagavad-Gita, a 700-verse Hindu scripture which is part of the epic Mahabharata, dated to the 2nd-century BCE. Many great thinkers from our times, such as Albert Einstein, Mahatma Gandhi, and Albert Schweizer, as well as Madhvacarya, Sankara, and Ramanuja from bygone ages, have all contemplated and deliberated upon its timeless message. The primary purpose of the Bhagavad-Gita is to illuminate for all of humanity, the realization of the true nature of divinity; for the highest spiritual conception and the greatest material perfection is to attain love of God! Based on the current events that are happening in the world, you feel like the future is uncertain and that the world is ending up being a sad place. Rather than thinking about the negative things that are going on in the world, make a positive impact in the world we live in by embracing and spreading love, peace, and unity to others. If we can all come together and do our small part each day in spreading love, peace, and unity, we can make the world a positive place for all of us to enjoy without any fear or sadness.

"World peace begins with inner peace."
—Dalai Lama

As I reflect back, **know your true self, purpose in life, take action, build and learn from experience, and meditation** had been guiding principles of my journey so far.

My early childhood village life was full of celebration of the festivals throughout the year, quite full of love and excitement. **The whole family**

was dependent on my father. I remember my father would be very busy being a provider for such a large family. I do not recall any incident when he played with his own kids. We were literally raised by my aunts and uncles; my father had four sisters and four brothers. After my grandfather's death, my grandmother took the command. My mother would get up early at 4:00 a.m., took a shower, and started with the household chores, including grinding fresh wheat to make flour to be used later in the day for all three meals for our large family. She would wake me up in Brahm Mahurat (Creator's time) with a kerosene lamp for me to start my studies, as there was no electricity in my village. **I can never forget the hard work my parents put in raising a family with sacrifice, selfness, peace, care, and tenacity.**

My First Pair of Shoes

Being raised in a joint family and being one of the youngest, I developed some very powerful skills that I was able to use later in my professional life. I learned such things as resilience, persistence, and waiting for your turn. This way, there was never any wastage of clothing or books; actually, there was never enough. One dress or uniform would be used by the person next in line whom the clothes would fit. Nursery to class five, I went to a government school in my village where we had to carry a mat to sit on, as there was no furniture to sit on. In the sixth grade, the school was in the nearby town, only a few kilometers away from my village, but at that age, it felt miles away. I was excited to walk on the road to the school, as in my village, we only had mud roads. I remember requesting my mother and giving the outline of my feet size on a piece of paper, which she had passed on to my grandmother; only after my grandmother approved, my father brought the very first pair of shoes. The whole night, I could not sleep, keeping my shoes under my pillow and kept waiting for the first light and get ready to go to school. What a feeling! **Confident, grateful, and blessed.**

Today, as I reflect back and see what made me successful, I identified with what Dwayne Johnson said: ***"I'm always asked, 'What's the secret to success?' But there are no secrets. Be humble. Be hungry. And always be the hardest worker in the room."***

Being an engineer: No dream is too BIG

At an early age, I would wonder why a human being weighing less than a couple of hundred pounds can't fly, but a plane, which is made of metal, which is not only huge but heavy, can fly. One day, an engineer came to our village for a large tubewell installation by the government. Government officers were provided a Jeep as a mode of transportation. Since no one in my village could answer my query, I asked the engineer my question, and he knew the answer and became my hero. He went on to share with me that you need to study hard, and only then you become an engineer and be able to know how things like this work. An engineer can build roads, bridges, buildings, planes, and motor cars. **At the age of thirteen, I knew what I wanted to be: *an engineer***. As I reflect back on the most interesting and exciting part of my life is being able to help reimagine—and create—the future. I strongly believe mankind is much better off because of the work and advancements by fellow engineers. They invent, design, analyze, build, and test machines, complex systems, structures, gadgets, and materials to fulfill functional objectives and requirements while considering the limitations imposed by practicality, regulation, safety, and cost.

"The best way to predict your future is to create it."
—Abraham Lincoln

Abroad education, moving to America: never settle for less

"We often settle for what's available, and what's available isn't always great. You are destined to achieve greatness!"
—Farshad Asl

After coming to Delhi from my village for higher education, I truly had a tough time. The new medium of education was in English, but I had only learned the English alphabet at the age of twelve, just five years ago. I faced many problems being a Hindi medium student, such as the slow speed of learning in the classroom of English medium courses and not being able to express my thoughts and ideas, hesitating during group discussions, etc. I had to first comprehend the topic in Hindi and later reproduce it in English, which required twice as much effort compared to other students. That really made me work harder than others.

I felt, at some point along my journey, I had lost sight of my goals and settled for less. I always wanted to go to the best school, the Indian Institute of Technology (MIT of India). I could not qualify for it. I was frustrated and became resentful, especially when I saw my friends in better schools. I wasted one year in Delhi and the following year got admission in Civil Engineering at Jamia Millia. Since I could not get admission to the top engineering college in India, I was disappointed with myself and developed resentment, which led to mental stress and unhealthy relationships with others. As I started knowing people, I made friends, and I overcame bitterness and later, time spent at Jamia became one of the best times of my life.

In the pre-final year of my engineering, two things happened, very coincidental, though. One, I came across an autobiography of Lee Iacocca, where he talked about his early childhood and going to Lehigh University. Second, I met Seema, my wife, who used to live in Bethlehem, the city where Lehigh University is located. This university is recognized among the nation's premier research universities, especially for civil engineering (environmental), my area of interest.

Seema and I got married two years later and moved to Bethlehem, but Lehigh was not a cheap school to go to. I got the Stafford loan of $7,500, admitted to one class. At Lehigh, I had the privilege of having Dr. Sibel Pamucku as my advisor on an environmental remediation project. I worked as a research assistant at Fritz Engineering Laboratory of Lehigh University on "utilizing scrap tires and iron slag in highway pavements." The materials investigated under this study were scrap tires in the form of Crumb Rubber Modifier (CRM) and iron process residue aggregate referred to as Iron-Rich Material (IRM). Today, I'm proud to share that my research work is helpful in many applications, including highways, parks, running tracks, playgrounds, etc.

SWADESI (COMING TO HIS OWN COUNTRY) RETURNS: MAKE A DIFFERENCE!

Becoming an engineer and entrepreneur was my childhood dream. After our son, Aman, was born, Seema and I started our first company in Silicon Valley in 1999, AstroWix Corporation, to help organizations unleash their potential using global best practices of project, program, and portfolio management. Within a few months into our entrepreneurial journey, Ashima, our beautiful daughter, was born in Fremont, California. **The dream of giving back to the motherland came true when Seema, the kids, and I moved to India, where we helped Microsoft and PMI establish project management culture and eco-systems in India.** To describe its success in the word of Mr. Gregory Balestrero, CEO of the Project Management Institute (PMI), "We owe it all to entrepreneurs like Upendra for not only setting the foundation but also of taking initiatives like this to give back more than what they have gained from their motherland." We had the privilege of working with some phenomenal people from whom we learned a lot and helped transform the lives of more than 100,000 professionals in more than twenty-five countries, including senior government and corporate leaders, including chairmen, vice-chairmen CEOs, IAS and IPS officers, director generals, commissioners, and various other officers of senior rank from e-governance reform, police reform, irrigation reform, smart city, infrastructure reform, and postal reform over a decade in India.

In 2009, I r**eceived the prestigious Eric Jennet Award by PMI® for the Outstanding Contributions to Global Portfolio, Program, and Project Management Profession in 2009 made me the first Indian and youngest professional to be bestowed with this honor**.

This would not have been possible without the deep rooted values, virtues, and beliefs inculcated in me at an early age.

Now, we live in Silicon Valley and miss India. I am fortunate to have Seema and kids and their love, care, and support. Staying in India with kids was a very exciting time where kids learned and experienced family values, relationships, and thousands of years-old rich culture.

Over the last few years, lots of effort has been put into unlearning, relearning, and realignment. Aman and Ashima had been awesome teachers who are continuously helping me to slow down, don't rush, and live in the movement. Seema is continuously looking for ways to improve the quality of our lives and goes on the road less traveled. She inspires me to go beyond what I can comprehend to level up and become a better version of myself.

Although life has been full of experiences and learnings, three learnings that stand out for me are:

1. Never settle for less

Although the adage to "never settle" is often used in relationships, but I found its application in every sphere of our life. Most people settle for jobs they don't love and don't pursue their passion. I chose to live life on my terms, always stretched my limits, created my own economy, and raised my standards always. I truly lived the words of Nelson Mandela, who said:

"There is no passion to be found playing small—in settling for a life that is less than the one you are capable of living."

2. You are the creator of your destiny

I strongly agree with the saying, "your destiny is in your own hands." Your reality is built out of your thoughts, so remember how much power you have. What you think, you become, what you feel, you attract, what you imagine, you create. We are responsible for what we are, and whatever we wish ourselves to be, we have the power to make ourselves. If what we are now has been the result of our own past actions, it certainly follows that whatever we wish to be in the future can be produced by our present actions, so we have to know how to act. Live your potential; time is finite. Act *now*!

3. Being in flow state for self-mastery

Over the years, I realized that self-mastery raises your level of consciousness by being in control of the internal thought processes that guide your emotions, habits, and behaviors. Developing self-mastery can radically improve your performance.

Self-limiting, fear-based mindsets that produce negative emotions also limit performance. They distract focus and confidence. When I reflect back on my past, I outperformed when I was centered and got into the inner state of the "flow" or "zone," key to performing optimally. When you increase your self-mastery, you improve all aspects of your life, both personally and professionally.

Self-mastery is captured well in this quote attributed to many:

."Watch your thoughts, they become words;
watch your words, they become actions;
watch your actions, they become habits;
watch your habits, they become character;
watch your character, for it becomes your destiny."

Self-mastery is not easy and requires hard work on patience, truthfulness, purity, impeccability, and faith.

I am a lifelong learner on this journey! Learning agility is the name of the game. Where the rules are changing fast, your ability to be agile in letting go of old rules and learning new ones is increasingly important. Learning agility is the key to unlocking your change proficiency and succeeding in an uncertain, unpredictable, and constantly evolving environment, both personally and professionally. Learn, unlearn, and relearn is my evolution mantra!

Upendra Giri

Simply put, Upendra is a transformer. Someone who is really passionate about transforming individuals, teams, and organizations to doing what they do better. He is an author, coach, trainer, and serial entrepreneur who helps senior leaders from the Bay Area to Bengaluru transform their organizations to achieve more innovation, collaboration, and business agility. At present, Upendra is CEO and Founder of UpLyft Global, committed to helping individuals, teams, and organizations on their transformation journey. Upendra has been instrumental in laying down the foundation of project management in India. In 2009, he was awarded the prestigious Eric Jennet Award by PMI® for his outstanding contributions to the global portfolio, program, and project management profession. He is the first Indian and the youngest professional who has been bestowed with this award to date. A true leader, evangelist, and professional engineer, he is also the founder and trustee of PMI® North India Chapter and is a charter member of TiE. Upendra earned his MS in civil (environmental) engineering from Lehigh University, Pennsylvania, USA, in 1994 and B.Sc. in civil engineering in 1991 from Jamia Millia Islamia University, New Delhi, India. Born in 1969 in a village in northern India, Upendra now resides in Silicon Valley, US, and is one of the most sought-after consultants by CEOs of big multinational companies and also an inspiration for budding entrepreneurs.

Website: **https://www.upendragiri.com** and **https://www.UpLyftGlobal.com/**
LinkedIn: **https://www.linkedin.com/in/upendragiri/**
Facebook: **https://www.facebook.com/upendra.giri.752**

THE NEXT STEP
BY ASHIMA GIRI

In the previous book, *Break Free To Stand in Your Power*, I talked about my story and my struggles with high school, depression and anxiety. How it led me to starting my own clothing brand that advocates for mental health, suicide prevention and how it's a safe space for people who are currently struggling.

Since I talked about my experiences with mental health as a teenager, I thought it only makes sense to talk about how I've been dealing with my mental health problems as an adult. **Transitioning from a teenager to adult was tougher than transitioning from a kid to a teenager. There are so many expectations by the world and yourself as an adult.** The world completely changes, you constantly have to think about so many things but mainly it's "how am I going to survive in this world?" and "what am I going to major in and what is going to make me money so that I'm completely relying on myself and not struggling?" Those are very hard questions that the answers can be only answered by yourself. When I first started my college career, I thought I wanted to major in Psychology and find a job in that field that could provide me with the life I want. But, by the end of the second year I realized that Psychology isn't for me and I don't know what else interests me. I decided Psychology isn't for me because it caused me nothing but stress and anxiety which made me look within myself. **Like everyone else, I want to do something that excites me everyday and that gives me something to look forward to. Other than my clothing brand and dance, I haven't felt like that towards anything else.**

Most people my age have figured out what they want to do, and some people that have lived a good chunk of life are just as lost as me in this big world. Day by day, I can feel myself disassociated from society and the material things don't mean as much to me as they used to. But, I still need to figure out what I want to do in life so I can make money to thrive and have fun. During times like this, I wished that the society and the world didn't need money to run on and all our basic necessities were met without the concept of money and restrictions. After thinking like that, I come back to my senses and once again I'm just as lost as I was when I first started. I look at the endless majors and nothing is as exciting as wanting to make clothes and sell them. But even with that, I'm lost. **The best case scenario is making money doing what you love and the worst case scenario is doing something you don't like as much and making money. Financially I will be fulfilled but emotionally? I don't think I will be fulfilled or as fulfilled.** What I end up doing for a living is something that fulfills all my needs like meeting my essential and non-essential needs. After a lot of evaluation and tests, I have found my strengths and the areas I excel in. After looking at that, I looked at other values and tried to look for a major that will include all those and will be very helpful to me. I decided on UX Design. It gives me the perfect area to grow in, I get to use my leadership skills that I have acquired, I get to be creative and work with a team. And getting a job in UX Design is very likely right out of college and it also pays well. I found something that will fulfil all my needs from spiritual level to being a citizen of the society level. It will also help me make my clothing brand into a company and bring it to the next level.

Now, going through the motions and going through this process was very hard on my personal mental health and it affected a lot of my areas like my personal relationships, my creative area, my relationship with myself. This area was a huge question mark, it felt like I was moving forward but moving forward where? My parents were doing everything they could to help me but ultimately it was up to me where to go and what to do. I was working on it trying to figure out what to do. But, on the outside, it didn't look like it so every time someone would talk to me about it, I would break down meaning I would lash and need time alone. Knowing the tools and using them to not fall back into depression was very helpful. These are the physical things I did that helped me a lot: I made sure I got some sort of exercise in, I regularly kept cleaning my room and my bathroom because I knew if I let it go, it will take a while to get back in and clean and feel better so I made sure those two things were being cleaned regularly. It also gave me something to do. I made my bed every morning. **I know it's small and mundane tasks but getting those things done made me feel less of a failure and more of a productive person. The point of getting everyday things done is being able to cross things off of the to do lists which gives you a sense of accomplishment.** Which makes you feel like you're doing something which will eventually lead to you doing more things that will help you get to your end goal. **Small things really do matter.** Emotionally and mentally, I journaled, I watched and researched things I can do better to improve my psyche, I did other activities that were stress releasing rather than stress inducing. I shifted my focus and indulged myself in whatever it was I was doing. I started looking at what I was eating and I started eating healthier, it helped a lot both physically and mentally. **What you put in is what you get, that's with literally anything. That concept can be applied to anything you do in life. When you look at what you've done so far and where do you want to go, what do you see?**

How do you feel? **The one thing I learned is that planning your future should be fun and exciting rather than exhausting and draining.** Yes, it can be stressful but what matters is how you deal with the stress. **One good tip is if the future you're planning doesn't excite you, that's**

probably not the path you should be on and that's okay. The society we live in makes us think we're way behind in life while others are moving faster than us. Everyone's timing is different. Also, the chances are whatever you major in won't be the thing you do 10 years from now. But, it doesn't make it less scary, it's hard. It's easy to get sucked into the toxicity of the whole productivity culture. **Yes, being productive is good but you don't have to be productive 24/7, 365 days. Take time off, refresh. It is very good for you. You need to. You're a human being not a machine. You are meant to have good and bad days. Just cause bad days exist doesn't mean you have to be scared and act all positive all the time**. Once your mind and body are refreshed, don't get sucked into the whole cycle again. Take time for yourself everyday even if it's 5-10 mins. If you are struggling with any mental illness, if you can seek professional help. Therapy is looked down upon because people don't want to be labeled as "crazy" but just cause you seek therapy doesn't mean you are. That's part of the stigma that we have to break. If you are not able to seek professional help then call the Suicide Prevention hotline (1-800-273-8255). It's not therapy but it's something, it's an outlet for you to talk about what's bothering you and now you can even text them.

Remember that you come first in your life and everybody is second so when it comes to planning your future, don't rush into it. Other people's advice matters but at the end, everything else is up to you. You matter. You are important and you are loved by others and most importantly by yourself. Make sure that you are happy with your decision at the end of the day.

Ashima Giri

Ashima Giri is a 20-year-old college student and the owner of a clothing line advocating for mental health awareness and suicide prevention called Don'tDieClothing (don't die clothing). Twenty percent of the profits go to suicide prevention organizations like San Francisco Suicide Prevention, The Trevor Project, and National Suicide Prevention Lifeline. The purpose of the brand is to let people struggling with any mental illness know that they are not alone and that there's hope. She was only 17 years old when this clothing brand was born and have impacted teenagers across the country.

Website: **www.dontdieclothing.com** and **AshimaGiri.com**
Instagram: **https://instagram.com/__dontdieclothing**.

Inspirational Quotes

Peace

"Letting go gives us freedom, and freedom is the only condition for happiness. If, in our heart, we still cling to anything—anger, anxiety, or possessions—we cannot be free." —Thich Nhat Hanh

"Peace is not only better than war but infinitely more arduous." —George Bernard Shaw

"When the power of love overcomes the love of power, the world will know peace." —Jimi Hendrix

"While you are proclaiming peace with your lips, be careful to have it even more fully in your heart." —St. Francis of Assisi

"Never be in a hurry; do everything quietly and in a calm spirit. Do not lose your inner peace for anything whatsoever, even if your whole world seems upset." —Saint Francis de Sales

"The life of inner peace, being harmonious and without stress, is the easiest type of existence." —Norman Vincent Peale

"Do not let the behavior of others destroy your inner peace." —Dalai Lama

"Nobody can bring you peace but yourself." —Ralph Waldo Emerson

"If you are depressed, you are living in the past. If you are anxious, you are living in the future. If you are at peace, you are living in the present." —Lao Tzu

"When things change inside you, things change around you." —Unknown

"Peace can become a lens through which you see the world. Be it. Live it. Radiate it out. Peace is an inside job." —Wayne Dyer

"When you have the courage to be *you*, you stop the internal war of how things should be and find the eternal peace within." —Seema Giri

"Focus on inner engineering for peace, love, and unity before you do outer engineering!" —Seema Giri

"Imagine all the people living life in peace. You may say that I'm a dreamer, but I'm not the only one. I hope someday you'll join us and the world will be as one." —John Lennon

"Peace comes from being able to contribute the best that we have, and all that we are, toward creating a world that supports everyone. But it is also securing the space for others to contribute the best that they have and all that they are." —Hafsat Abiola

"Peace is not the absence of conflict; it is the ability to handle conflict by peaceful means." —Ronald Reagan

"Not one of us can rest, be happy, be at home, be at peace with ourselves until we end hatred and division." —John Lewis

"When you make peace with yourself, you make peace with the world." —Maha Ghosananda

"Do your little bit of good where you are; it's those little bits of good put together that overwhelm the world." —Desmond Tutu

Love

"We accept the love we think we deserve." —Stephen Chbosky

"Love takes off masks that we fear we cannot live without and know we cannot live within." —James Baldwin

"The most important thing in life is to learn how to give out love and to let it come in." —Morrie Schwartz

Self-Love

"If we give our children sound self-love, they will be able to deal with whatever life puts before them." —Bell Hooks

"I think forgiveness is probably one of the greatest forms of self-love there is because you don't do forgiveness for anybody else." —Elizabeth Smart

"Self-love is the source of all other loves." —Pierre Corneille

"Self-love is really a foundation for everything, and however you practice or express that is so, so important." —Solange Knowles

"The deepest gift you can learn in life is about self-love." —Rumor Willis

"Self-love has very little to do with how you feel about your outer self. It's about accepting all of yourself." —Tyra Banks

"Loving yourself isn't vanity; it is sanity." —Andre Gide

"Had we not loved ourselves at all, we could never have been obliged to love anything. So that self-love is the basis of all love." —Thomas Traherne

"I think the most important thing in life is self-love, because if you don't have self-love and respect for everything about your own body, your own soul, your own capsule, then how can you have an authentic relationship with anyone else?" —Shailene Woodley

"Self-love is an ocean, and your heart is a vessel. Make it full, and any excess will spill over into the lives of the people you hold dear. But you must come first." —Beau Taplin

"You yourself, as much as anybody in the entire universe, deserve your love and affection." —Buddha

"When I loved myself enough, I began leaving whatever wasn't healthy. This meant people, jobs, my own beliefs, and habits—anything that kept me small. My judgment called it disloyal. Now I see it as self-loving." —Kim McMillen

"It's surprising how many persons go through life without ever recognizing that their feelings toward other people are largely determined by their feelings toward themselves, and if you're not comfortable within yourself, you can't be comfortable with others." —Sidney J. Harris

"Most of the shadows of this life are caused by standing in one's own sunshine." —Ralph Waldo Emerson

"The reward for conformity is that everyone likes you but yourself." —Rita Mae Brown

"It's all about falling in love with yourself and sharing that love with someone who appreciates you, rather than looking for love to account for a self-love deficit." —Eartha Kitt

"Did your mom ever tell you, 'If you can't say something nice, don't say anything'? She was right—and talking nicely also applies when you're talking to yourself, even inside your head." —Victoria Moran

"Accept yourself, love yourself, and keep moving forward. If you want to fly, you have to give up what weighs you down." —Roy T. Bennett

"When we fulfill our function, which is to truly love ourselves and share love with others, then true happiness sets in." —Gabrielle Bernstein

"Self-esteem and self-love are the opposite of fear; the more you like yourself, the less you fear anything." —Brian Tracy

"Love yourself first and everything else falls into line. You really have to love yourself to get anything done in this world." —Lucille Ball

Unity

"Unity is strength ... when there is teamwork and collaboration, wonderful things can be achieved." —Mattie Stepanek

"The essence of the beautiful is unity in variety." —W. Somerset Maugham

"Coming together is a beginning. Keeping together is progress. Working together is success." —Henry Ford

"So powerful is the light of unity that it can illuminate the whole earth." —Baha'u'llah

"Once the realization is accepted that even between the closest human beings infinite distances continue, a wonderful living side by side can grow, if they succeed in loving the distance between them which makes it possible for each to see the other whole against the sky." —Rainer Maria Rilke

"The most important thing in life is to learn how to give out love, and to let it come in." —Morrie Schwartz

"Love will find a way through paths where wolves fear to prey." —Lord Byron

"If I know what love is, it is because of you." —Herman Hesse

"I love you not because of who you are but because of who I am when I am with you." —Roy Croft

"Love is a friendship set to music." —Joseph Campbell

"We are shaped and fashioned by what we love." —Johann Wolfgang von Goethe

"When we are in love we seem to ourselves quite different from what we were before." —Blaise Pascal

"Love in its essence is spiritual fire." —Seneca

"The way to love anything is to realize that it may be lost." —Gilbert K. Chesterton

"It takes courage to love, but pain through love is the purifying fire which those who love generously know. We all know people who are so much afraid of pain that they shut themselves up like clams in a shell and, giving out nothing, receive nothing and therefore shrink until life is a mere living death." —Eleanor Roosevelt

"Don't brood. Get on with living and loving. You don't have forever." —Leo Buscaglia

"We are only as strong as we are united, as weak as we are divided." —J.K. Rowling, *Harry Potter and the Goblet of Fire*

"I offer you peace. I offer you love. I offer you friendship. I see your beauty. I hear your need. I feel your feelings. My wisdom flows from the Highest Source. I salute that Source in you. Let us work together for unity and love." —Mahatma Gandhi

"Within sorrow is grace. When we come close to those things that break us down, we touch those things that also break us open. And in that breaking open, we uncover our true nature." —Wayne Muller

"In order to have a winner, the team must have a feeling of unity; every player must put the team first—ahead of personal glory." —Paul Bryant

"For the strength of the Pack is the Wolf, and the strength of the Wolf is the Pack." —Rudyard Kipling

Peace, Love and Unity

"When I say it's you I like, I'm talking about that part of you that knows that life is far more than anything you can ever see or hear or touch. That deep part of you that allows you to stand for those things without which humankind cannot survive. Love that conquers hate, peace that rises triumphant over war, and justice that proves more powerful than greed." —Fred Rogers

Happiness

"The seed of suffering in you may be strong, but don't wait until you have no more suffering before allowing yourself to be happy." —Thich Nat Hahn

“My actions are my only true belongings.” —Thich Nat Hahn

“Our own life has to be our message.” —Thich Nat Hahn

“I promise myself that I will enjoy every minute of the day that is given to me to live.” —Thich Nat Hahn

Humanity

“You must not lose faith in humanity. Humanity is an ocean; if a few drops of the ocean are dirty, the ocean does not become dirty.” —Mahatma Gandhi

“There is a nobility in compassion, a beauty in empathy, a grace in forgiveness.” —John Connolly

“Compassion for others begins with kindness to ourselves.” —Pema Chodron

“There is no exercise better for the heart than reaching down and lifting people up.” —John Holmes

“You have not lived today until you have done something for someone who can never repay you.” —John Bunyan

“I have just three things to teach: simplicity, patience, compassion. These three are your greatest treasures.” —Lao Tzu

Resilience

“On the other side of a storm is the strength that comes from having navigated through it. Raise your sail and begin.” —Gregory S. Williams

"Only those who dare to fail greatly, can ever achieve greatly." —Robert F. Kennedy

"Our greatest glory is not in never falling, but in rising every time we fall." —Confucius

"When we learn how to become resilient, we learn how to embrace the beautifully broad spectrum of the human experience." —Jaeda Dewalt

"Resilience is very different than being numb. Resilience means you experience, you feel, you fail, you hurt. You fall. But you keep going." —Yasmin Mogahed

"It's your reaction to adversity, not adversity itself that determines how your life's story will develop." —Dieter F. Uchtdorf

"Note to self: every time you were convinced you couldn't go on, you did." —Unknown

"Courage is not the absence of fear, but rather the judgment that something else is more important than fear." —Ambrose Redmoon

Life

"Regulate your mind. Do not worry excessively about the future. If you have done everything that has to be done, the future will take care of itself." —Master Choa Kok Su

"Life is like an echo! when you give something, it comes back to you many, many times." —Master Choa Kok Su

"When I uplift myself, I lift others around me." —Seema Giri

Author Poems and Quotes

"I promise a world of we where we all live in peace, harmony
And prosperity.
I believe unity is power
We all work together regardless of differences.
We empower each other with loving-kindness, empathy and
Respect.
We create a world of truth goodness and beauty as a source
For a future of the power of we."
—Marsha Cheung Golangco, "The Power of We"

"We flow down the mountains Soul; fill up the ocean Spirit and it never overflows our bodies always return." —Karina Aragon

"Whenever you find yourself on the side of the majority, it is time to pause and reflect. Kindness is the language, which the deaf can hear and the blind can see. Patriotism is supporting your country all the time and your government when it deserves it. Don't let schooling interfere with your education. Courage is resistance to fear, mastery of fear, not absence of fear." —Mark Twain

"Be different, be kind." —Karina Aragon

"What you think you become. What you feel you attract. What you imagine you create." —Buddha (Sharon Caren's favorite quote)

K is for knowing the right thing to do
I is for inspiring others to follow you,
N is for never forgetting the cue
D is for displaying it in whatever you do,
N is for not always getting it right
E is for ensuring you try with all your might,
S is for sorry when you do get it wrong
And S yet again to remain strong. —Una R. Lappin, "Kindness"

B is for the BRAVERY we use each and every day
R is for the RESPECT we all deserve in each and every way,
E is for the ENERGY we have, use and desire
A is for the APPRECIATION we all work to and aspire,
T is for the TIMING we take for others each day
H is for the HOME we have, kept in our own special way
And E is for EMPATHY we all try to achieve, in living this life as we breathe.
—Una R. Lappin, "Breathe"

Empathy

"Empathy is the gift of compassion. It opens the door to inspired understanding despite apparent differences and leads to peaceful and empowered cooperation between people. Its pathway is through a forgiving Heart by letting go of our past disappointments and wounds and by embracing our Divine Nature as the loving and enlightened Souls that we truly are."
—Yvonne Mughal

Closing Thoughts

Dear amazing reader,

I hope you enjoyed and were touched by these powerful chapters. Each author carefully handpicked stories from challenging times in their lives so they could inspire, educate and empower you to realize your brilliance. To give you a sense of hope and encouragement, and let you know you are not alone.

We can't wait for you to break free to peace, love and unity and celebrate as you share your heartfelt love and compassion with the world.

I would like to share additional resources that may be supportive as you progress in your healing or awakening journey.

The first is my podcast, **Break Free to Brilliance,** where my guests share their experiences of breaking free, finding their genius and their gifts of brilliance they've shared with the world, and how they stood in their power.

You can find the weekly
podcast episodes here

https://www.seemagiri.com/podcast/

If you want even more clarity, support and accountability as you navigate to your **new "normal,"** I offer several workshops, group programs and personal coaching.

1. *The Authorities* is my first anthology with *New York Times* best selling author, Dr. John Gray, from the *Mars/Venus* series. My chapter is called "Break Free from Your Pain Cycle," in which I share my journey from being bedridden to living life on my terms. Available on Amazon.

2. Group Coaching: **Break Free to Brilliance**
   A 16-week program for women entrepreneurs and leaders who:
   - Feel burned out, overwhelmed and exhausted
   - Want to live life to the fullest
   - Reclaim their body, mind and soul to live in the flow of their passion by building a strong wellness foundation.

3. Master Classes
   - Meditation
   - Wellness
   - Shine Your Brilliance as an Author
   - Take Charge of Your Future

4. We are continuously coming up with new, free resources to help you navigate how you want to move forward. You can find them at www.seemagiri.com

5. One of key catalysts in turning my health around has been whole food supplements and the tower garden. You can find more information at www.seema.juiceplus.com or www.seemagiri.com

If you are ready to shine and share your story of breaking free from challenges and living life on your terms, and if you are ready to help others stand in their power, you can participate in our upcoming anthologies and podcast.

If you would like to personally connect with me to explore opportunities in my programs, podcasts and book writing projects, then schedule a time with me at http://bit.ly/TalkwithSeema, or you can email me at seema@seemgiri.com

May you always STAND IN YOUR POWER!
Sincerely,

Seema Giri

"There are two primary choices in life: to accept conditions as they exist, or accept the responsibility for changing them."
—Dennis Waitley

What choices are you making?

Made in the USA
Monee, IL
26 April 2021

66429183R00095